·DECORATIVE·

PAINT FINISHES

CREATIVE HOMEOWNER PRESS®

CONTENTS

COPYRIGHT © 1994 CREATIVE HOMEOWNER PRESS®
A DIVISION OF FEDERAL MARKETING CORP.
24 PARK WAY, UPPER SADDLE RIVER, NJ 07458

Based on *Creating a Home, Paint Finishes for Home Decorators*

First Edition © Eaglemoss Publications Limited, 1986

Printed at Webcrafters, Inc. Madison, WI, USA

Current printing (last digit)
10 9 8 7 6 5 4

Editorial Director: David Schiff
Editor: Alexander Samuelson
Cover Design: Annie Jeon

Library of Congress Catalog Card Number: 94-71875
ISBN: 1-880029-38-3

Photo Credits:
Front Cover
Martin Senour Paints, Cleveland, OH (top left)
Grand Illusion Decorative Painting, New York, NY (top right and background)
Jackie Shaw Studios, Inc., Smithsburg, MD (3rd down, right)
Page 1 Grand Illusion Decorative Painting, New York, NY
Page 2-3 Trevor Richards- Homes & Gardens- Robert Harding
Back Cover
Elizabeth Whiting & Associates (top and bottom)
Henry Bourne- Homes & Gardens- Robert Harding (middle)

INTRODUCTION

The current popularity of those special-effect paint finishes which were once the province of the professional decorator has encouraged more and more people to try their hand at these traditional techniques.

Decorative paint finishes proves that even the homeowner can master the skills needed to create a wonderful variety of effects on walls and doors, floors and furniture. An exciting alternative to plain paint or wallpaper, many of these finishes are extremely practical, too, providing a handy disguise for uneven walls, giving a new look to a tired decorating scheme, and adding a touch of class to ordinary furniture.

From straightforward sponging through to more ambitious tortoiseshelling, each technique is fully explained. Color photographs illustrate each step and small-scale projects suggest ways of trying out your new-found skills. If mixing colors is not your strong point, there are plenty of design hints to help you make your choice.

For the absolute beginner, the early chapters cover some of the simplest and quickest paint finishes: sponging, ragging, colorwashing and, most fun of all, spatter painting! Their random appearance makes them the ideal choice for a first attempt since small irregularities tend not to show.

Dragging, stippling and combing are just some more of the more adventurous finishes you will be inspired to try. In addition, there are 'fantasy effects' – surprising look-alike techniques that can give a wooden floor the feel of marble, a dull picture frame the luxury of tortoiseshell!

Ever popular and infinitely versatile, the art of stencilling gets the coverage it deserves, with three chapters and full-size patterns for you to trace to make your own stencils.

Not for the faint-hearted, the final chapters show how you can have fun with freehand painting, transforming old furniture and shabby household objects into original works of art!

Ragging and rag rolling

*A scrunched up rag rolled in parallel lines or
dabbed over a wet paint surface creates a decorative design on
walls, ceilings and furniture that echoes moiré or
crushed velvet. Ragging gives a random pattern, while rag
rolling is used for a more regular effect.*

Ragging and rag rolling are simple and quick to do and require little equipment. The subtle patterns can look more interesting than plain walls without imposing on the decor of a room as some wallpaper designs do. Both techniques are ideal for disguising uneven or blemished walls. They can also be used on furniture; but rag rolling should only be done where the repeat pattern will show up.

A variety of effects

Effects can be delicate or dramatic. For example, using two colors at the same time gives a subtle effect, while leaving one coat to dry before applying the next creates a more striking contrast.

▽ *The subtle effects created by ragging add warmth and texture to the walls of a dressing room.*

Preparation

Rags become clogged and need replacing as you work so have a number ready cut. An ideal size is about 8in (20cm) x 12in (30cm). Use rags of the same material to complete the job as a change in fabric will show up in the design. When you are cutting up the rags, remove all hems, seams and stitched areas, as these will spoil the finished paint effect.

The rag material and the colors you use both decide the strength or subtlety of the pattern. To make sure that you will be happy with the result, it is a good idea to do some samples on white poster board first. Tape these in position on the surface to be decorated and check the effect in both day and night light before making a decision on which technique to use.

△ *Rolling is most effective over large areas as it produces a consistent repeat pattern. This makes it perfect for use on walls and ceilings.*

△ *Ragging forms a random design which creates an all-over effect. It is ideal for use on small areas such as baseboards, chairs and tables.*

A successful finish

While ragging, it is best to change the position of your hand to avoid the creases in the rag creating a design that is too repetitive.

When rag rolling, make sure that you fold the rag so that there are enough creases to create the right effect. It is best to turn in the rag ends and loosely crumple it in your hands. The rag will form a sausage shape when rolled up the wall.

Rag rolling gives a regular repeat pattern but the rag-rolled lines do not need to be straight; a slightly wavy line often gives the best effect. The lines must be vertical – if they go off at an angle they will be very noticeable.

On a large area such as a wall, establish your first rag-rolled line by using a plumb line and bob. This gives you a straight edge to follow, and is the best guide as you cannot

◁ *Ragging is the perfect technique for decorating country homes. The random swirls create a rustic atmosphere which complements the wooden fireplace and floral chairs.*

Method

First, the surface is painted with a semi-gloss base coat and allowed to dry thoroughly. A glaze is made up by mixing a second color, or a deeper or lighter tone of the first, with an oil glaze. This is then painted over the base coat. While this is still wet, a clean, scrunched-up rag is used to make the design.

Ragging involves dabbing the wet glaze with the rag, while rag rolling requires the rag to be rolled up the wall in vertical lines, each just overlapping the previ-ous one. The rag removes some of the wet glaze from the surface and, depending on which technique you have used, reveals the base color beneath in either a regular or random design.

The glaze must be worked on before it starts to become tacky. You can do ragging or rag rolling on your own, although rag rolling especially is best done by two people. The oil glaze is applied by one person working down the wall in a strip, while the second fol-lows behind forming the design with the rag.

△ *A crumpled rag is rolled up the wall in one movement, forming a stripe. The process is repeated, overlapping the pattern slightly each time.*

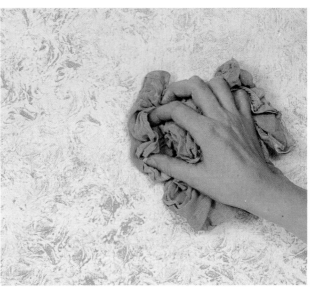

△ *A rag is loosely scrunched up and patted over the prepared wall, removing the glaze in patches. This reveals the color beneath, creating a mottled print.*

mark the wet wall. You will only need to do this once as repeat lines are not difficult to keep vertical; they will simply follow the direction of the first one.

If a ragged area is splashed while applying the coat of oil glaze to a nearby area, just dab the mark so that it blends in. If the glaze on any of the ragged areas is too thin, brush paint over this area and rag once more.

Color combinations

When planning your color scheme, bear in mind that the best results are created by using a lighter shade as the base color and ragging or rag rolling a darker shade over the top. Create extra interest by reversing the colors in some areas; for example, use light colors over dark on mantelpieces and shelves.

The safest way to achieve a suc-cessful result is to combine two tones of the same color; for exam-ple, try ragging terra cotta over burnt umber for a warm look, or use a deep sky blue over a pale blue for a cooler effect. By experiment-ing with color combinations you can create different moods and effects: lemon yellow over citrus green will produce a vibrant scheme, whereas cream on golden yellow will be sub-tle.

Try ragging pale grey or blue over white for a pastel scheme, or aqua on light green for a tranquil effect. Alternatively, rag apricot over cream for a more cozy feel. To create dramatic contrasts, try navy or wine on a white background, or use pale blue over poppy red.

Materials

Rags

Cotton is the traditional material for producing this finish, and old cotton sheets are ideal. To rag roll an average size room 12ft sq (3.65m sq), you need one torn up single sheet. A fabric made up totally from man-made fibers is not suitable as it will not absorb the paint. However, fabric that contains a small proportion of synthetic fibers, such as a cotton-polyester, works well. Experiment with differ-ent materials; for example, chamois, linen and cheesecloth.

Transparent oil glaze

Transparent oil glaze slows down the drying process of the paint. It also helps to give the top coat a transparency impossible to repro-duce in any other way. It can only be mixed with oil-based paints (those that can only be removed from brushes by using turpentine).

TIP	SAFETY

Ragging or rag rolling a room will leave you with a lot of paint-clogged rags. Ensure that these are dry before throwing them away as rags still soaked in wet paint are a fire hazard. After using turpentine, ensure that its lid is firmly screwed on, and that it is in a safe place out of childrens' reach.

A striped bathroom

The beautiful and unusual appearance of this bathroom is created by rag rolling subtle grey stripes over a magnolia base.

You will need

◇ 4in (10cm) paint brush
◇ Semi-gloss paint in base color
◇ Semi-gloss paint in top color
◇ Transparent oil glaze
◇ Turpentine
◇ Paint bucket for mixing glaze
◇ Rags cut into squares
◇ Plastic sheets or newspapers
◇ Rags for mopping up
◇ Rubber gloves
◇ Plumb line and bob

1 Prepare the surface by filling any cracks and holes with patching compound. Brush on the base coat and leave to dry. If there is a contrast to the color underneath, you may need to apply two coats. Allow to dry well.

2 Using a plumb line and bob, mark straight lines down the wall a distance of about 8in (20cm) apart. Protect the areas that aren't going to be rag rolled by covering with masking tape.

3 Make up the glaze from 20% grey eggshell oil paint, 70% oil glaze and 10% turpentine. Sand the base coat lightly to ensure that the paint will adhere, and wipe down with a rag dipped in turpentine.

4 One person should apply the top coat of paint using long, vertical brush strokes, while the other follows along, rag-rolling from the bottom to the top.

△ *The subtle colors of this rag-rolled design add an air of freshness and height to a bathroom.*

5 Stand back and check that the ragging design covers the stripes evenly. If there are any spaces in the pattern, fill in by lightly touching up with the rag.

▽ *The rag-rolled stripes on the wall emphasize the vertical wooden panels. The panels themselves have been rag-rolled in the same way for a coordinated finish.*

Sponging

Walls, woodwork, furniture and accessories can all be transformed with this attractive paint effect. Partly covering the surface, it allows a toning or contrasting base color to show through. This type of finish is also an excellent disguise for slightly uneven surfaces.

What is sponging?

This is a quick and easy technique in which one or more colors are applied with a slightly dampened sponge over a solid base color. A natural sponge is best; a synthetic sponge can be used if you tear it to an irregular shape and apply the paint with the inner surface.

You can create subtle or striking results depending on the colors you choose, the spaces between the sponge marks and the size of the sponge. It is usual to sponge a darker color over a lighter base but it is quite possible to work the other way around.

Contrasting colors give dramatic effects whereas closely related tones will create a more subtle textured finish. Sponging with just one color can look rather 'spotty', unless the sponged color is closely related to the base coat – apricot on warm yellow, for example.

In general, two or more sponged colors give a more pleasing effect than one. Always try out various color combinations before starting work on a project. It is advisable to have a few strips of poster board to experiment on; keep these efforts and a note of the colors for reference later.

Materials

Latex and oil-based paint

For beginners, it is a good idea to experiment first with latex-based paint only. Latex is a water-based paint and is much less trouble to prepare and to clean up. When you are confident, you can progress to using oil-based paints and transparent oil glaze.

Transparent Oil Glaze

Traditionally, broken paint effects have been created using oil glaze. This commercial product is a transparent glaze which is tinted with artists' oil-based paints or Universal

Sponging a tray

A simple wooden tray makes a good starting project for sponging

You will need

◇ 4in (100mm) paint brush
◇ Latex base coat/sponging coat
◇ Thinner – water
◇ Scrap paper for testing
◇ Shallow dish
◇ Natural or synthetic sponge
◇ Plastic sheets/newspapers
◇ Rags for mopping up
◇ Rubber gloves
◇ Polyurethane gloss (optional for sealing the finished tray when using latex based paint.)

1 Rubber gloves	4 Thinners
2 Natural sponge	5 Shallow dish
3 Paint brush	6 Paint

4 Lightly dab the sponge over the surface. Turn the sponge as you work in order to vary the pattern. If you are sponging with just one color you should keep the marks fairly close together. If you are using two or more colors you can space them out a little more.

5 Load the sponge with paint whenever necessary, testing it on a piece of scrap paper each time before recommencing your work. Re-start sponging in a corner or inconspicuous place in case the new sponge mark blurs. If you start in the middle of an area, it might be obvious if the first sponge marks were too heavy.

tints, then applied over an oil-based base coat (usually a semigloss paint such as eggshell). Since the glaze is semi-transparent, even when tinted, it allows the base color to glow through, giving a rich warm finish to walls, woodwork and furniture.

Sponging different surfaces

As a rule you should not mix different types of paint. Remember always to use oil-based on oil-based paints and water-based on water-based paints.

For sponging on walls, you can use latex paint. Applying the base coat is easy using a roller. For the sponged coat, paint can be applied straight from the can. However, you will achieve a softer color effect if you dilute the paint with a little water.

On small items, woodwork, or in kitchens and bathrooms, which are subject to heavy condensation, semi-gloss oil paint is a good choice. Before sponging, thin the second oil color with a little turpentine to make the coverage easier.

| TIP | PUTTING IT RIGHT |

◇ A less-than-perfect result can easily be improved. If you have sponged on too much color, sponge on a little of the base coat.

◇ You can give a too-subtle effect more impact by adding a considerably darker shade or a lighter shade or even a contrast color.

1 Prepare the surface of the tray and paint on the base coat. Leave to dry thoroughly.

2 Pour a little sponging color into a shallow dish. Dip the sponge into water and squeeze it thoroughly. Then dip it into the paint and squeeze to remove excess paint.

3 Experiment with the color on scrap paper to discover the sort of effect you want – try the paint diluted or straight from the tray to see which provides the best results. Keep dabbing until the sponge leaves a soft speckled mark. The sponge should be almost dry so that the marks show; if it is too wet the paint will blur or run.

6 Apply a second sponged coat when the previous one is quite dry. Fill in gaps between prints and also overlap some to blend the colors.

▷ *The base color for the tray is very pale apricot; the first sponged color is Wedgwood blue and the second is soft peach.*

7 Polyurethane gloss can be applied over the final sponge coat when it is dry.

COLOR LIBRARY

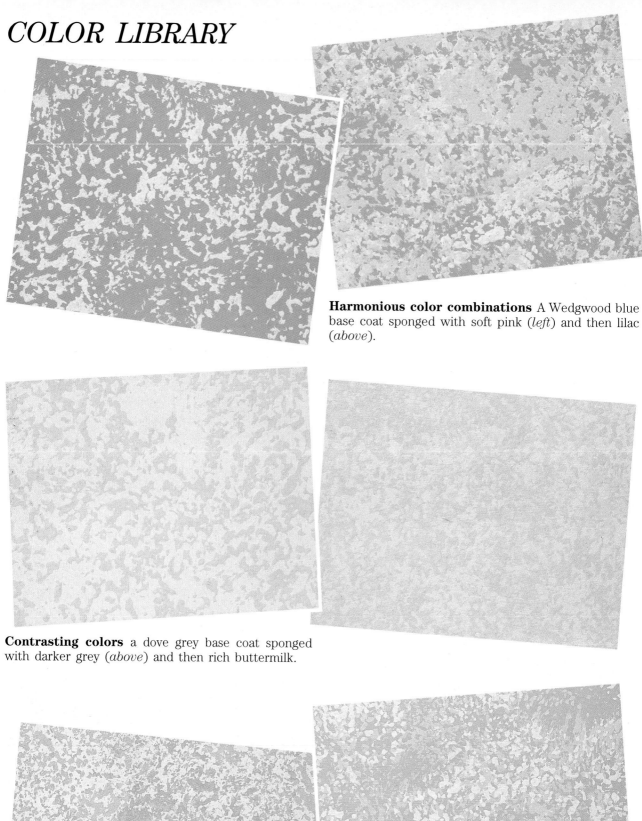

Harmonious color combinations A Wedgwood blue base coat sponged with soft pink (*left*) and then lilac (*above*).

Contrasting colors a dove grey base coat sponged with darker grey (*above*) and then rich buttermilk.

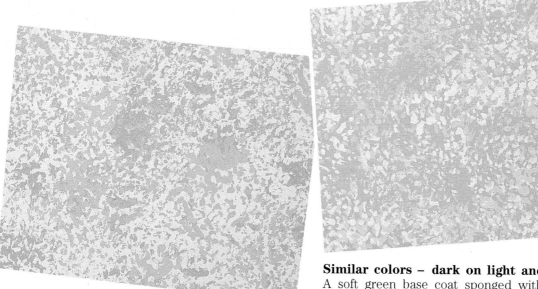

Similar colors – dark on light and light on dark
A soft green base coat sponged with medium green then dark green (*left*). The order is reversed (*above*).

Colorwashing

*'Colorwash' is a broad term used to describe any
decorating technique that involves painting one color over
another so that the base color shows through.
Before the days of pre-mixed household paints, diluted lime
tinted with pigments was used for colorwashing.*

The secret of successful colorwashing is confidence and bold brush strokes. With these two vital ingredients, even beginners can achieve stunning results. Once you have started painting a wall or other surface, keep going: never try to touch up or go back over what you have already done as small irregularities will not show once the work is finished.

The best colorwashes are produced by painting a transparent glaze over a base color and then partially removing it to reveal the color beneath. Diluted latex and other household paints can be used instead of glaze, but they are more difficult to apply and less effective because they lack the translucent glow of real glazes.

The technique of color washing is best suited to large areas such as walls, doors or big items of furniture. This is because the glaze is usually partially removed with a dry brush, using large random strokes. These sweeping strokes on a small surface are less effective and can be difficult to achieve. A cloth can also be used too remove the glaze, but this method is restricted to large areas of wall or ceiling in a room.

▷ *Be adventurous in your
choice of colors for
colorwashing. It is possible
to use much bolder colors
than you would normally
choose, as a rich glaze will
be softened by a paler base.*

Materials and equipment

Base color

When choosing colors, the base coat is as important as the top coat of colored oil glaze because it shows through the loose brush strokes and transparent glaze, affecting the final color. A white base gives a light, airy look to the finished wall. A deep base color creates a darker, intimate effect.

Glaze

Use a water-based, latex glaze over an acrylic or latex base coat, and an oil glaze over a semi-gloss oil base. For colorwashing, the glaze should be heavily diluted to a very thin, watery consistency. For further detail on glazes and information on the proportions used for making transparent glazes, see pages 9 and 24.

Brushes

An ordinary paint brush can be used for applying the base and the glaze and for removing excess glaze. Alternatively, to produce a more textured effect, a specialist brush, such as a dragging brush or over-grainer, with widely spaced, tufted bristles, can be used to remove the glaze. A dry cloth gives a similar effect; see page 25.

Colorwashing

The following demonstrations used an oil-based semi-gloss base and an oil-based glaze. The glaze was made by mixing equal proportions of oil glaze and turpentine. Artists' oil paints were used to color the glaze.

Basic colorwash technique

1 Using a paint brush, apply the glaze solution to the base color with loose brush strokes.

2 While the glaze is still wet, take a dragging brush and go over the surface with quick random strokes to remove some of the paint.

Two-color effect

When two colors are used they combine to make a third color. By 'mixing' colors on the wall you can achieve beautiful effects of broken color with flecks of the base color showing through, instead of the flat, opaque look of pre-mixed colors.

1 Here, a bright yellow oil glaze is brushed over a strong magenta oil glaze. The result is a vivid glowing orange color with flecks of yellow and magenta showing through in places.

2 Soften the glaze color by working over the surface with a dry dragging brush in the usual way.

Pattern and texture

You can create surface patterns by controlling the direction of the brush strokes. Wavy lines, criss-cross strokes and diagonal trellis patterns, for example, add interest to a large expanse of plain wall.

1 Apply the colored oil glaze to the oil base coat in the normal way.

2 While the glaze is wet and workable, use the dragging brush in various directional strokes to create the pattern of your choice.

A softening effect

For a more delicate, finer texture, slap the surface of the glaze, while it is still slightly wet, with the flat side of the brush. The technique is slower but gives a softer textured effect than basic colorwashing. This method is most suitable for smaller areas, such as doors or pieces of furniture.

1 Apply the base coat; allow to dry completely. Then paint on the colored glaze.

2 Using a dry dragging brush or paint brush with long bristles, slap the flat side of the bristles sharply on the wet glaze to break up the brush strokes and remove excess color. Repeat this technique until you have covered the required area.

A striped effect

Although not a true colorwash, these stripes make a cheerful wall decoration using the same materials and techniques (see previous pages).

DESIGN IDEAS

1 Using two or more glaze colors, paint the stripes on to the base color of the wall.

2 Pull a dry dragging brush across the glazed surface in the same direction as the stripes to soften the edges.

△ *A rich creamy yellow base, topped with a soft gold glaze gives a warm glow.*

◁ *An aqua glaze over an off-white base forms a lively backdrop for this unusual panelled bath.*

Spattering

*Spattered paint is effective, easy and fun to do.
Whether you are painting a tiny object to give it a fine, multi-
colored texture, or decorating a large piece of
furniture or a wall, spattering gives a lively, cheerful finish
that can brighten and enhance any type of surface.*

Spattering is very straightforward to do and the effect can be achieved with the most basic of materials. Most of us have spattered paint by accident and hastily mopped up the result. But deliberate spattering – building up droplets of paint to produce a textured surface pattern – is very creative and can produce beautiful, decorative results. An old brush or toothbrush and some paint are all you need to produce this versatile paint finish.

Materials and equipment
Paints
Almost any type of paint can be used for spattering, depending on the surface you are decorating. Whichever paint you choose, it should be mixed to the consistency of thick cream. Test the mixed paint before using it. If it is too thick the paint will tend to stick to the brush; if it is too thin it will form rivulets of color and spoil the spattered effect.

Artists' oil paint is ideal for spattering and should be diluted to the right consistency with turpentine. Oil paints can be used on top of an oil-based paint, with a gloss finish. They are slow-drying and the paint should be allowed to dry before removing any masks to avoid smudging the spattered texture.

Artists' paint When working with these quick-drying paints, mix only as much paint as you can use in one session as left-over paint dries hard and is wasted. Acrylics need to be diluted with water. They should not be used on top of an oil-based paint because the oily surface will eventually repel the acrylic paint and so spoil the finish.

Latex water-based paint For painting and spattering large areas, household latex is economical and comes in a wide range of colors. But, like acrylics, it should not be spattered on top on an oil-based paint as the latex will be repelled by the oily surface.

Craft paints Enamels, fabric paints and ceramic paints, should be diluted with the appropriate solvent. Follow the manufacturers' instructions regarding suitable surfaces.

Brushes

Spattering is usually done with a toothbrush or a small paint brush, depending on the size of the area to be painted. For wide expanses use a 2-in paint brush or a large artists' brush. For small objects and fabric painting an old toothbrush is ideal because it allows more control over the final texture.

Surfaces

Suitable surfaces for spattering include fabric, walls, plastic, metal, wood, paper and porcelain. Obviously, the nature of the surface dictates the type of paint you choose, but all surfaces must be clean and well prepared before being decorated.

Spattered colors look best when applied over a flat color. So a wall painted with flat latex, a plain fabric item or a piece of painted furniture are all ideal for decorating using the spattered paint technique.

Masks and stencils

Masking tape, paper masks and stencils can all be used to protect areas which are not to be painted. For straight lines and geometric shapes, masking tape is the most effective method, but you can also use cut-out stencils and torn paper as well as a variety of other flat shapes. For example, leaves, feathers and paper doilies have all been successfully used as alternative stencils for spatter painting.

Mixing color

Mix enough color for the job you are doing before starting to spatter. It is almost impossible to get exactly the same shade if you do run out of color, so be sure to mix plenty at the outset. Use clean vessels, brushes and mixing sticks and store the paint in screw-topped jars for future use.

Toothbrush spattering

1 Place strips of masking tape on work surface to form desired shape; protect surrounding area with paper. Then load the toothbrush with paint: either paint it on to the toothbrush with a paint brush or dip the bristle tips in a shallow container of paint. Hold the loaded toothbrush a few inches from the surface and draw your thumb firmly backwards across the bristles to release the paint.

2 Apply the second and any subsequent colors in the same way. If you are using the same toothbrush for each color, make sure it is well washed and dried between each color – working with a wet toothbrush causes the spattered paint to run.

3 When the paint is dry, carefully lift the masking tape at one corner and pull it upwards away from the painted surface.

Paint brush spattering

1 Use the jagged edge of a torn sheet of paper as a mask to produce an irregular shape. To create a coarsely textured effect, apply the spattered paint with a paint brush. Dip the tips of the bristles into the paint. Then, holding the brush handle firmly in one hand, sharply tap the side of the brush against the side of your other hand to disperse the paint in large spatters over the surface.

2 Further colors can be added in the same way. To achieve a dense, heavy effect, hold the brush close to the surface; alternatively, for a lighter, sparser texture, lift the brush several inches clear of the painted surface.

3 When the paint is dry, carefully remove the mask from the spattered surface.

TIP   USING MASKS

◇ For geometric shapes, use masking tape to block areas not to be spattered. Press down the edges to prevent paint seeping underneath.

◇ Spattered paint covers a wide area, so protect the surrounds of the masked shape with sheets of paper or newspaper, taping them in place if necessary.

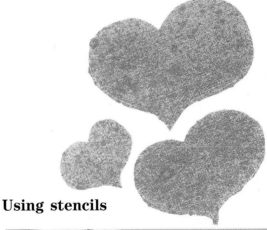

Using stencils

1 Choose a simple design and trace it onto a sheet of stiff paper, stencil film or cardboard. Protect work surface with a cutting mat or heavy cardboard and cut out the shapes with a razor knife.

21

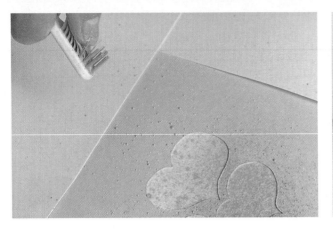

2 Lay the stencil on the surface to be decorated and protect the surrounding area with sheets of paper. Spatter the color over the cut-out design.

3 Leave the paint to dry completely, then carefully remove the stencil.

Mugs and tablecloth

Make tea time a colorful occasion with these coordinated mugs and tablecloth. Nothing could be simpler than this geometric pattern which borders the cloth and the white mugs. You could also decorate napkins and other items of tableware using the same motif.

You will need

◇ White mugs
◇ Plain white tablecloth
◇ Masking tape
◇ Fabric paints (pink, yellow and blue) and solvent
◇ Ceramic paints (pink, yellow and blue) and solvent
◇ Old toothbrush

Spattered mugs

1 Mask off the design by running two parallel strips of masking tape along the top of each mug, approximately ½in (1.2cm) apart. Join these at regular intervals with short diagonal strips of tape. Protect the rest of the mug with tape.

2 Mix each ceramic paint color to a creamy consistency, using the appropriate solvent. Use a toothbrush to spatter the paint.

3 When the paint is dry, remove the masking tape to reveal the multi-colored spattered border.

Spattered tablecloth

Lay the tablecloth on a flat surface and decorate in the same way, using the fabric paints. Use masking tape for the design, and protect plain areas of cloth with paper before starting work.

Dragging

The technique of dragging dates back to the 18th century, when it was used for wood-graining to produce a grain effect without actually exposing the bare wood. It is popular today as a decorative finish on doors, panels, walls, floors and larger pieces of furniture.

This traditional decorating technique is achieved by first applying a transparent or semi-transparent color over a different base color. Then, while the paint is still wet, a large, dry brush is 'dragged' across the surface with firm straight strokes so that the underneath color shows through.

Dragging gives an unusual and creative finish.

△ *These kitchen cupboards have been painted using the technique of dragging. They contrast well with the walls, which have been painted to achieve a marbled effect.*

Materials and equipment

Paints

Paints with two different finishes are used in dragging: the solid base coat and the transparent glaze which gives the grained finish. When choosing paint for dragging it is important to remember that there are two quite different types of paint – oil-based paints and water-based paints. The two types have different drying times and should never be mixed as they are totally incompatible. Also note that oil-based paint is followed by an oil glaze, but a water-based paint can be followed by either water or oil glaze.

Base color

If you intend to finish with an oil glaze, use an oil-based semi-gloss paint for the base coat. If you cannot buy exactly the color you want, it can be mixed to the correct shade using artists' oil paints or tints. When using a latex glaze, the base coat should be latex or acrylic.

Glaze

Oil glaze Available in cans, this is a thick, yellowish substance that resembles honey. Because the glaze has to be thin it should first be diluted with an equal quantity of turpentine.

Oil glaze can discolor slightly with age. This is not usually severe enough to be a great disadvantage, but it is sometimes noticeable with pastel colors.

This transparent glaze mixture can be colored with artists' oil paints or liquid tints to a strength to suit your chosen color scheme. Mix in the color thoroughly to prevent lumps of paint or tint spoiling the finished effect. One problem with oil glaze is that it is extremely slow drying – the process can take several days if the painted surface is in a cool room.

Latex glaze This is often used as a varnish to protect decorated finishes like polyurethane. When it is mixed with an equal amount of water, it can be used as a water-soluble glaze. Latex glaze looks white when wet but it becomes transparent when it dries. It can be colored with watercolor, gouache, artists' acrylic or tints. This glaze dries very quickly, making it unsuitable for use on large areas if you are working on your own. With two people, however, one person can apply the glaze while the other brushes the surface.

Brushes

The base color can be applied with an ordinary paint brush – choose a size suitable for the area you are working on.

To produce the grained effect, a dragging brush, sometimes known as a flogging brush is best. The bristles of these specialist brushes are very long and are arranged in tufts to give space between the lines of the dragged, paint effect.

Suitable surfaces

A dragged finish can be applied to most types of surface, although it is more difficult to get an even effect on small areas. Walls and household woodwork such as doors, baseboards, floors and large items of furniture are all suitable subjects for dragging.

Preparing the surface

The surface to be painted should be well prepared, clean and free from loose particles. Wood should be rubbed down with sandpaper and new wood must be primed before applying the base color.

Dragging

The following steps show the basic techniques of dragging and how to achieve the wood-grained effect. We used an eggshell oil-based coat followed by an oil glaze. If you are using a latex or acrylic base coat with a latex glaze, follow the same basic steps.

1 Apply the base color with a large painter's brush. The surface of the base coat of paint does not have to be absolutely flat, but care is needed to avoid uneven patches which can often show through the glaze. Leave to dry thoroughly.

2 Mix the glaze with equal parts of oil glaze and turpentine. Add enough artists' oil paint to give you the color you want. Mix the solution thoroughly and then apply it to the dry base color.

3 While the glaze is still wet, take a dry dragging brush and drag this firmly across the glazed surface. Repeat this action, with the next strokes slightly overlapping the previous ones.

4 Confidence is important when using the dragging technique, if you are to achieve straight, bold lines that reveal the base color. Any hesitation will be reflected in the final pattern.

TIP   SMALL ITEMS

If you are working on a small object or in a confined area, it may be easier to do the dragging using a rag instead of a dragging brush.

1 Apply the base color as usual and leave to dry.

2 Scrunch up the rag and dip it in the transparent oil glaze mixture. Draw it over the surface in the same way as you would the brush.

Blanket box

Add a touch of color to a bedroom by dragging a plain wooden blanket box in the rich, russet hues of autumn colors.

You will need
◇ Wooden blanket box
◇ Pink semi-gloss oil paint
◇ Artists' oil paint
◇ Oil glaze
◇ Turpentine
◇ Paint brush
◇ Dragging brush
◇ Sandpaper
◇ Primer
◇ Varnish

1 Rub the blanket box down with sandpaper to roughen the surface and remove any loose particles of paint. The box pictured here is an old blanket chest. If you are painting a new box, with exposed wood, you will need to prepare it first with a coat of primer.

2 Paint the box with a coat of base color. If this looks patchy, you may need a second coat. Leave to dry.

3 Make the transparent glaze mixture (see step 2 of the basic technique). Add artists' oil paint to achieve the color of your choice.

4 Beginning with the larger, main surfaces first, paint the transparent glaze mixture over the base color. While this is still wet, drag the surface using the dry dragging brush. When this is complete, drag the edges of the lid in the same way, using the narrow side of the brush.

5 Allow the glaze to dry completely. For a professional finish, protect the surface with two coats of polyurethane varnish.

COLOR LIBRARY

△ *Create a warm, sunny look by dragging terracotta over an apricot base color.*

△ *This tranquil effect has been created by painting a peppermint green color over white.*

△ *Here, sky blue glaze has been dragged over a creamy-white base color.*

△ *Alternatively, try dragging two colors, one over the other in opposite directions over the base coat.*

Stippling

*Stippling involves dabbing a flat-faced brush
on a wet, colored glaze to lift speckles of glaze off
the surface and allow the base coat color to
show subtly through. Furniture, walls and doors can all be
transformed with this delicate, flecked finish.*

This ever-popular technique of stippling combines two separate colors, one painted on top of the other, to give a soft paint effect. Despite the subtlety of the finished effect, this technique enables you to create a rich and exciting depth of color that cannot be achieved with 'flat' coats of paint.

Materials and equipment
Stippling brushes
A specialist stippling brush is square in shape and has flat, fairly stiff bristles. It is rather costly, but creates a uniform effect. Stippling brushes come in a wide range of sizes – from those with a large surface area of bristles, to small, narrower ones. Choose a small brush for stippling furniture and a larger

A successful finish
Unlike sponging or ragging, which can conceal poor surfaces, stippling needs a smooth base; any unevenness will be highlighted. The paint glaze must be applied evenly, then the brush should be dabbed firmly on to the surface, working in vertical stripes. Do not try to cover too large an area at once; experiment on a small area first.

Stippling is easier if two people work together; one to apply the glaze and one to stipple it off. But make sure that there is no change in who brushes and who stipples, as any change is likely to show. Use a rag to clean the brush if it becomes saturated with glaze – but do not use turpentine part way through as this can cause the paint to run.

Stippling a filing cabinet
The smooth surface of a metal filing cabinet is ideal for stippling. This technique, worked in a color to coordinate with its surroundings, will transform an ugly piece of furniture into a far more attractive item.

You will need
◇ 2in (5cm) paint brush
◇ Primer for metal
◇ Oil paint in two colors
◇ Transparent oil glaze
◇ Turpentine
◇ Rubber gloves
◇ Sandpaper
◇ Medium size stippling brush
◇ Plastic sheets or newspaper
◇ Rags for mopping up
◇ Polyurethane gloss varnish

3 Mix the top coat glaze using the correct proportions of the second oil color, the transparent oil glaze and the turpentine.

4 Paint the glaze, applying it in vertical stripes over the side of the cabinet.

size for decorating walls.

Alternatively, experiment with any brush that has bristles of an even length, such as a shoe cleaning brush. A mohair or lamb's wool roller creates a similar, but softer and less defined look. On small areas, a flecked effect can also be achieved by using a synthetic sponge or a square of carpet.

Mixing the glaze

Use a mixture made up of 70 percent transparent oil glaze, 10 percent turpentine and 20 percent oil paint (in the color of your choice) for the top coat.

First of all, mix the oil color separately with a little turpentine (add a small amount of white primer if you want to lighten the tone, or to stop it yellowing when added to the glaze). When you are satisfied with the color, it can then be added to the glaze and stirred until well mixed.

Before mixing colored glaze for a large area, test a small amount on a sheet of white paper.

Color choice

Strong colors are a good choice for stippling, with one rich color being used over another; a wine red stippled over bright pink creates a beautiful, warm look. Or try working royal blue over turquoise, for a more sophisticated effect.

Working a deep color over white also looks effective: for example, stipple emerald green or bright yellow on white for a bright, fresh appearance. Do not use two pale or closely related colors over each other, as the effect of the stipple will be lost.

If the base is a light color, stippling a deep glaze over the top will have the effect of softening and at the same time strengthening the base coat. For example, the overall effect of stippling a deep blue over white is mid-blue on pale blue. Alternatively, a room decorated in too strong a color can be toned down by stippling a paler shade over the top. This effect was very popular during the 1930s.

1 Sand the surface and paint with a coat of primer suitable for metal. Leave to dry. Then lightly sand the surface to create a surface the paint can grab.

2 Brush on the oil paint as a base coat. Allow the paint to dry thoroughly, sand again, and brush on a second coat. Leave to dry.

5 Starting from the base, and working upwards, stipple one side of the cabinet with a firm, jabbing movement. If you cause a streak, re-coat the mark with glaze and stipple over it.

6 After one side is finished, stipple the surface opposite to it in the same way. (This will help to prevent smudging the first side.) Continue in this way until all the surfaces are stippled.

7 Allow the paint to dry out completely for two days and then coat the stippled surface with clear, polyurethane varnish.

COLOR LIBRARY

△ *Emerald green stippled over a white base color.*

△ *Royal blue stippled over white.*

△ *Deep wine stippled over a sharp pink color.*

△ *Terracotta stippled over gold.*

△ *White stippled over emerald green.*

△ *Cream stippled over terracotta.*

Crackleglaze effects

*When one type of paint or varnish is mixed
with another type, the two surfaces work against each
other to produce a pattern of hairline cracks
on the surface. This technique can be used to mimic age or
simply for its decorative appeal.*

It is now fashionable to reproduce the lovely, subtly crazed surface found on old pieces of furniture, oil paintings, or even walls and doors. Layers of paint or varnish can be used to create this effect. With the varnish method a water-based varnish is applied over an oil varnish, causing the surface to crack. The cracks can be highlighted by rubbing oil paint into the surface. Crackle varnish can be used on a plain painted surface or on a patterned surface, which will be visible beneath the varnish.

The crackle paint effect works on a similar principle, with the top layer cracking to reveal the layer beneath. Use subtle colors to age furniture or bold colors to pro-duce purely fun effects. Both the crackle varnish and crackle paint techniques are covered here.

Traditional causes

The crazed surface on old painted furniture or oil paintings was formed either by the varying drying times of the materials used or by changing atmospheric conditions.

Oil paintings are a good example of the effect of varying drying times. The paint takes much longer than the protective varnish to dry, causing the varnish to crack.

In time, changes in temperature and humidity also cause painted surfaces to crack. Dust then lodges in the cracks, highlighting them and increasing the effect of age.

Crackle paint effect

This broken color technique can be used to blend newly painted items with favorite, older, worn pieces of furniture. Alternatively, use it as a fun, decorative effect.

A base coat of one color latex is painted on the surface and then covered with a layer of transparent gum arabic. Gum arabic is the magic ingredient that persuades the top coat to split open. When this has dried, a second color latex is brushed over it.

Speed is essential as the water in the paint soon softens the dry gum arabic. To work, the layers must stay separated. The top layer starts to crack immediately to reveal the base color in streaks and speckles.

What to decorate

Any item which can be painted is suitable, but you must experiment with colors and technique before you start. Use the finish to decorate door or cupboard frames, lamp bases, candle sticks and enamelware jugs. Do not use it to paint containers that are used for food, as water-based paint will not stand up to regular washing.

Color choice

This finish looks most effective when contrasting colors are applied, or when it is used to show off different tones of one color. Bear in mind that the streaks and splatters of the background color may be lost if they are too subtle.

Materials and equipment

Latex paint Ordinary household latex paints (those thinned with water) can be used.

Gum arabic Most art shops sell water-color gum arabic. You can also buy crystals which need to be dissolved in boiling water and then left to stand overnight to thicken slightly. Crackle paint kits, which include gum arabic, are available from large art and craft shops.

Protective finish As both methods end with a water-based layer, some protection is needed. The first part of the two-part crackle kit can be used as a final protective coating. Or use polyurethane varnish in matt or satin finish.

Crackle paint method

You will need

◇ Latex paint in two colors
◇ Paint brushes, about ½ wide
◇ Water-color gum arabic

2 Add a small bit of water to the gum arabic to stop it breaking open when applied; mix thoroughly. Brush the gum arabic over the entire surface and leave to dry.

1 Prepare the surface of the item to be painted so that it is clean, dry and completely free from grease. Apply a coat of the first color latex and leave to dry thoroughly.

◁ *The smaller items have all been painted using the crackle technique, while the door behind, cracked with age, was highlighted with a new wash of paint.*

▽ *Some of the crackle paint effects possible.*

3 Quickly and evenly paint a second color latex-acrylic over the surface. Do not go over the same area more than once as this will mix and spoil the previously applied layers. Cracks start to appear very quickly – use a hair dryer to speed up the process and to make bigger cracks in the top layer of paint.

4 For a finer crackled finish, repeat steps 2 and 3. Finally, varnish or wax the surface to protect it from wear and tear.

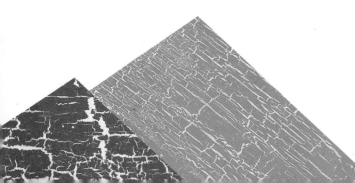

Crackle varnish effect

Newly painted or restored items stand out harshly against those 'aged' by time. Methods have evolved to copy the effects produced naturally over years, to lessen the contrast between old and new.

The first cracking varnish was patented by two French brothers in the 18th century. They discovered that by using varnishes with varying drying times – a quicker drying water-based varnish over a slower drying oil-based one – the top dry layer would crack as the lower layer moved while drying.

What to decorate

Crackle varnish can be used to age any paint-decorated surface, such as small items of furniture or picture frames. It also works well as a finish for decoupaged objects.

Materials and equipment

Crackle varnish is available in a two-part pack, which contains two different varnishes. The slow-drying oil-based varnish is used first. The quicker drying water-based varnish is then brushed over the top. The pack is available from large art shops. You can make your own crackle varnish using an oil-based and water-based varnish. Experiment first, in case you do not achieve the required effect.

Artists' oils are rubbed into the surface to highlight the cracks. For an aged effect use dark, earthy colors like raw umber or burnt sienna. For a more modern look choose strong, bright colors.

The oil paint, mixed with a little turpentine, is rubbed lightly over the surface using a cloth. By going over the surface with a clean cloth excess paint can be removed, leaving a small amount in the cracks.

Crackle varnish method

You will need

◇ Crackle varnish pack (or two types of varnish: one oil-based and one water-based)
◇ Two paint brushes, about ½-1in wide
◇ Artists' oils for highlighting the cracks
◇ Turpentine
◇ Lint-free cotton rags

1 Thin first coat of varnish with turpentine, if necessary, so that you can brush it over the surface in a thin, very even layer. Leave to dry until the surface is just tacky when you touch it – this usually takes 1-2 hours, but can vary according to the temperature and humidity of the room you are working in.

2 Quickly cover the entire first coat of varnish with a thick layer of the second, water-based varnish. Leave to dry. The cracking becomes more obvious if you use a hair dryer to speed up the drying process.

▷ *This tray was painted and limed, and then 'aged' using the crackle varnish technique. The cracks were defined with artists' oil paints.*

3 When the varnish is dry, and if you are satisfied with the finish, continue to Step 4. If the cracking is too subtle, the first layer of varnish was too dry when the second coat was applied. In this case, wipe off the second varnish with a damp cloth and repeat steps 1 and 2, leaving less time between applying the coats.

4 Mix the chosen artists' oil color with a little of the first

coat of oil-based varnish. Using a rag, rub this gently over the entire surface and work it well into each of the cracks.

5 Using a clean, dry cloth, carefully remove the excess oil color from the surface, leaving some in the cracks.

6 Allow final finish to dry for 3-7 days. Protect with two coats of oil-based varnish or wax.

Watercolor washes

*Transform a room by painting the furniture
in delicate pastel shades. These subtle effects are produced
using a watercolor paint wash – the color gently
tints the furniture to give a translucent look. This easy
technique produces surprisingly stylish results.*

By coordinating the decor of a room, you can produce a feeling of balance and harmony. Here a folding screen, two stools, a chest of drawers, and various boxes and plates have been decorated with a paint wash using delicate pastel shades to produce an overall feeling of light and tranquillity.

The color wash for the furniture is made by tinting inexpensive white, flat, latex paint, first diluted with water, then with colored inks or artists' watercolor paints. This makes it possible to make a wide range of colored paint washes for the cost of just one can of paint.

Experiment with color

It is important to experiment with the colors you are going to use. This will enable you to make sure that each piece of furniture not only complements the others but also fits in with its surroundings.

An ideal and easy way to experiment with various color combinations is to use paint sample color charts, which are readily available from paint stores. Simply place different charts next to one another to see which colors work well together.

When planning the color scheme, take into account the existing colors and patterns in the room. You could, for example, pick out some of the colors in a patterned sofa or curtains. Or you might be inspired by the colors in a favorite picture or poster.

Materials and equipment

Little equipment is needed for these projects. Most of it, such as bowls, saucers and spoons for mixing paint, can be borrowed from the kitchen.

White water-based paint is used as the base ingredient for the color wash. Water-based paints, give a softer, more subtle effect than oil paints (which are much brighter and harder in tone because they reflect more light). To make the paint wash, a white matt finish is used as the base and diluted with a lot of water. Color variations are then made by mixing pigments – in the form of gouache or inks – into the paint.

Gouache is an opaque, water-based paint which is sold in small tubes from artists' supply shops. It can be added to the diluted white paint to produce colored washes.

Colored inks are readily available from art shops and can be mixed with the diluted paint mixture in the same way as gouache to produce the colors of your choice. Colored inks give a more translucent effect than gouache.

Making a paint wash

All water-based paints can be mixed with varying amounts of water so that they are thick and creamy or very runny. For the techniques shown here, you need to mix the paints to a very runny consistency. If the paint goes lumpy when you are mixing it, or forms a rubbery skin on the surface, you can remedy this by passing it through an ordinary large kitchen strainer.

Spend some time just experimenting with mixing colors; this will help you to achieve the exact shades you desire. It will also reveal any do's and don'ts of paint mixing and will help you judge the quantities of paint needed.

TIP	VARNISHING

By their very nature, water-based paints are not waterproof. Therefore, any decorated surfaces which may come into contact with water – such as in a bathroom or kitchen – should be protected with a coat of matt glaze.

▽ *This studio apartment shows how it is possible to use a wide range of colors to decorate a room successfully. By carefully co-ordinating the tones and shades of a selection of colors, rather than just using a single color, you can create a wonderfully tranquil and harmonious overall effect.*

Pair of stools

The stools have been painted first with white, flat latex paint and then a colored wash. Use this method to paint any wooden items of furniture in your home – such as a small side table or a picture frame.

You will need

◇ White flat latex paint
◇ Water-based paints (either gouache or inks) in colors of your choice (we used bright red and cobalt blue)
◇ Sponge
◇ Spoon
◇ Flat varnish (water-based is good)

Method

1 If necessary, prepare the surface of each stool before painting: sand them down using abrasive paper and then paint them with primer/undercoat. Sand them down again to remove any brush marks. Then paint each stool with a coat of undiluted white flat latex paint; sand down again to provide a smooth surface for the color wash.

2 To make the basic watercolor paint wash, mix a small amount of white flat latex together with lots of water – as a rough guide, try adding 2 tbsp of paint to each gallon of water.

3 To produce a pastel tint, add a small amount of water-based paint (either gouache or ink) in a strong color to some of the diluted paint mixture. Add only a few drops of color at a time to each gallon of diluted paint. Add the color gradually for better control of the depth – it is easier to make a color darker than it is to lighten it.

4 When you are happy with the pastel shade you have created, sponge the mixture on the stools using a damp sponge (see pages 11-14).

5 Leave the tinted wash to dry completely. To protect the finish add a coat of matt varnish.

△ *While these stools have been painted for a practical use, the plates are purely decorative, giving you the opportunity to experiment with all your gouaches. (If you want to actually use these plates, you must use special ceramic paints.)*

Folding screen

Repeat the pastel theme by decorating an old screen to coordinate with the newly painted furniture. The screen is simply covered with a length of good quality watercolor paper, held in place with gummed brown tape. The splashes of color are added by painting an area of the paper with water, then adding a spot of gouache or ink, which diffuses to fill the area with soft color.

Practice the technique first on remnant scraps of watercolor paper. Dampen and stretch the samples of paper before starting to paint.

You will need

◇ An old wooden folding screen
◇ A roll of thick watercolor paper
◇ Sponge
◇ Thumbtacks
◇ Brown gum package tape
◇ Ruler and pencil
◇ Watercolor paints or inks in the following colors: green, moss, lime, orange, grey and pink
◇ 1 in paint brush
◇ Blotting paper or absorbent cloth

Preparing the screen

1 From the roll of watercolor paper, cut a piece long enough to cover each panel. Dampen it with a very wet sponge or carefully soak it in a bath tub.

2 Once the paper is thoroughly dampened, smooth it over panel, making sure there are no air bubbles between paper and wood. Fix in place using thumbtacks at corners and tape the paper around the edges of the wood. Leave to dry away from heat. It is important to soak and stretch the paper first to prevent it buckling when the paint wash is applied.

3 Draw a grid on to the paper, with each square measuring approximately 4in (10cm) across.

Painting the screen

1 Dip the paint brush into a glass of water and paint patches of water well inside pencil grid.

2 Dip the brush into the first color and dot it on one of the water spots. The color will run and gradually diffuse through the water spot, making a slightly brighter color round the edge. If necessary, use blotting paper or an absorbent cloth to soak up any excess moisture.

3 Repeat with the rest of the colors and allow to dry thoroughly away from any heat.

Chest of drawers

The chest has been painted with two washes – with a slash of white base coat left to divide the two colors. The handles are also painted in different pastel shades, chosen to complement the base colors.

You will need

◇ White primer
◇ White flat latex paint
◇ Gouache or ink (we used silver-grey and lilac)
◇ 2in (5cm) paint brush
◇ A sponge or lint-free cotton rag
◇ Masking tape
◇ Flat varnish

Method

1 If the chest has a wax finish, you should clean it with turpentine and then sand it before painting. Then paint the surface of the chest with white primer. Sand again to remove any brush marks.

2 Make up a diluted paint mixture, as for the stools (previous page, steps 2 and 3). Divide the mixture in half and make two separate pastel tints by adding the silver-grey to one and the lilac to the other.

△ *The pastel theme has been successfully repeated to decorate this folding screen. Although the screen has been divided with a very regular grid pattern, the actual splashes of color on each section have been cleverly used to create different effects.*

3 Carefully position the masking tape diagonally across the front and top of the chest of drawers (refer to photograph) to divide the chest into two triangular sections.

4 Dip the paint brush into the pastel lilac wash, and brush it over the area to right hand side of masking tape. Do not take the wash right up to the tape, thus leaving slightly ragged edges.

5 Repeat this, using the silver-grey wash, to paint the area to the left of the masking tape, again stopping the wash just before the edge of the tape. Gently wipe over the finish with a rag or sponge. Use matt varnish to protect the surface.

◁ *Leave a slash of white between two soft pastel washes to prevent the colors from merging into one. A finishing coat of matt glaze will help to protect the surface from any splashes of water – especially when watering any plants being displayed on top!*

Combing

*With its distinctive textured finish, combing is ideal for
disguising shabby walls, furniture and wood. Although traditionally
used to simulate wood grain, this technique is now
enjoying renewed popularity as a way of producing original
patterns and colors on all sorts of surfaces.*

This simple technique involves combing patterns into wet paint using a hard comb. A base coat is applied and allowed to dry. This is followed by a top coat which is combed while still wet so that the base coat shows through. The size and scale of the pattern is dictated by the size and spacing of the comb's teeth and to some extent by the material of the comb.

Combing is often referred to as a way of imitating or emphasizing the grain in woods. However, it can be quite difficult to re-create the natural, textured look of wood. The following few pages provide helpful, practical advice on the choice of combs available as well as demonstrating a variety of simple and more elaborate abstract combing designs that are much easier to achieve and are equally as effective.

Abstract combing

The strong lines produced by combing can also be used to create stripes, diagonals and patterns such as fans, waves and checks in a wide variety of colors and interesting textures.

Some combing patterns can be used successfully on large surfaces; for example, dull floorboards can be livened up with a strong wavy pattern in a natural color or, for real impact, in a bright and daring color. Alternatively, small objects such as trays, boxes or frames can be given a more delicate combing decoration with the use of a fan or check technique.

◁ *Old furniture, such as this chest of drawers, can be renewed with the addition of cheerful and original textured patterns. The chest was bought in a junk shop and combed in dramatic black on a white undercoat.*

Materials and equipment

Paints

Base coat On walls, the base color for a combed surface can either be water or an oil-based undercoat. On furniture and floors, use an oil-based undercoat.

Top coat The combed color should be an oil-based paint with a gloss or eggshell finish. This is slow drying and remains workable long enough for you to make the combed textures and patterns. You can also use thinned artist's oil colors – although these are quite expensive and very slow drying. Better still, translucent oil-based glaze, tinted with artist's oil colors provides a transparent combing color which allows the ground color to show through and adds another dimension to the finished effect.

To ensure a workable consistency your oil paint should be diluted with turpentine (up to 25 percent), but remember that the paint must be thick enough to hold the texture of the combed marks.

Varnish

When the combed paint is dry it is possible to apply added protection to the finish with a matt or gloss varnish. If you have used a gloss oil-based paint for the combed surface it is only necessary to varnish if the surface is to be subjected to the excessive wear and tear that might be expected in a bathroom or kitchen.

However, gloss varnish can be used as an additional decorative element which can give lift to the colors beneath the glassy surface.

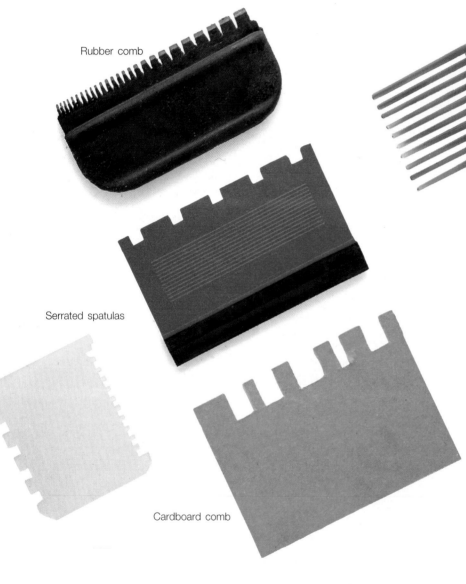

Rubber comb

Serrated spatulas

Cardboard comb

Hair pick

Combs

A flexible comb is used to make patterns; rigid materials can be used, but take care not to scrape and damage the base color.

Wood-graining combs These are usually made of rubber and come in a range of sizes. Some rubber combs have graduated teeth which produce a series of lines with varying widths and spaces.

Triangular combs are also available, which have the advantage of combining three different spacing options in one implement.

Steel wood-graining combs These must be covered with a thin, lint-free cloth before they are pulled over the paint surface.

Serrated spatulas Use the flexible plastic serrated type that comes with adhesives and fillers.

Hair picks Are effective because they have chunky, widely spaced teeth.

Alternatively, cut your own comb from stiff cardboard and seal it with a coat of varnish.

Wood-graining combs

Preparing surfaces

Plaster walls, wooden floors and furniture are all suitable for combing. It is not possible, however, to comb wallpaper with a raised pattern. New or unpainted wood should be primed before applying a base coat and new plaster should be left for at least six months to dry out before priming. Sand painted woodwork and fill any holes or cracks.

On uneven walls, the combed color and texture tends to be irregular. However, this can look attractive and be effective over a large area.

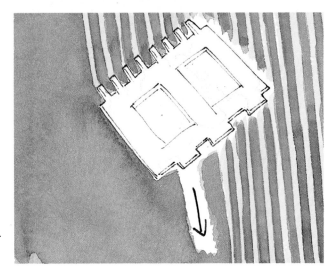

Combing surfaces

1 Apply an even base coat to the prepared surface. Leave to dry, then sand lightly and repeat if necessary.

2 Thin the top color slightly with turpentine (if it is too thick, you will get ugly, uneven ridges in the pattern) and brush over the base. Remember, once the paint starts to dry it cannot be combed, so work a manageable area at a time.

3 When using a fairly transparent paint (or glaze) there may be faint brush marks in the surface. On large areas these will not show; on small items you can remove them before combing by lightly dabbing the wet paint with a soft cloth.

4 Drag the comb through the wet surface to reveal the contrasting color of the base coat beneath, keeping your strokes as even as possible. You can vary the pattern by changing the direction of your strokes (see below).

5 Once you are happy with the pattern and have applied the desired layers of combing, it is important to leave the paint until it is completely dry. If necessary apply two thin coats of clear varnish to protect the textured surface.

Fan shapes

Of all the methods of combing that can be used, these fan shapes produce possibly the most dramatic, textured effect, particularly on smaller objects, as can be seen with this simple tray (below). The pattern is created by keeping one end of the comb in the same position and swivelling the other end around to form an arc (right). Further overlapping rows of arcs are then applied.

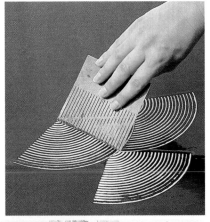

Color schemes

Choice of color will make all the difference to the final design. In order to achieve the right effect, the base color should be of a contrasting tone to the intended top coat color. In other words, if your combed color is to be dark, choose a white or pale base. Conversely, use a dark base under a light colored top coat.

For the more adventurous, it is possible to introduce subsequent colors into a combed design. This can be done by applying a second color over the first and superimposing another combed pattern – in which case, the second color will dominate. Alternatively, you can introduce random splashes of top coat colors on the first combing.

TIP	TRIAL RUN

Try out your paint first and experiment with the amount of turpentine you will need. The absorbency of the surface, the type of paint, even the weather will affect the way the paint can be worked.

41

PATTERN LIBRARY

Criss-cross zigzag A comb with graduated teeth is used to pull abstract zigzag patterns on top of one another, vertically and horizontally.

Waves Undulating and waving lines can be used on a large area, such as a floor surface, or as borders and edging patterns.

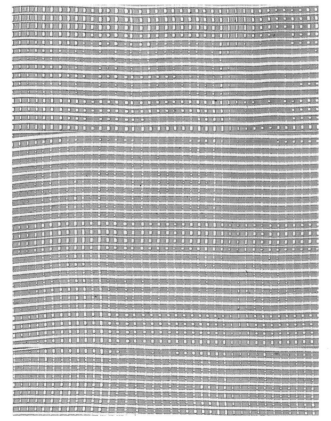

Fine criss-cross This is an easy way of creating a fabric-like effect on any surface. All you do is work horizontally and vertically with a fine comb.

Zigzag Pulling the comb backwards and forwards diagonally, changing direction sharply at each edge, creates an angular, zigzag pattern.

Using wood stains

Staining timber can bring out or improve the richness of a wood's natural color as well as enhancing the pattern of the grain. Newer semi-translucent stains widen the palette to include a rainbow of bright and pastel colors not seen in natural wood.

Wood stains are now available in a wide range of colors, opening up a whole world of decorative effects. By carefully choosing the right type of wood stain it is possible to transform the appearance of a wood floor or a piece of furniture to give them subtle color. It is also possible to give cheaper softwoods the appearance of more expensive hardwoods with stains in wood tones.

Wood stains can also be used to create a range of more unusual effects. You can, for example, stain different sections of a piece of furniture to create tonal contrasts or stain floorboards to mimic beautiful, more costly woods.

Stunning effects can be created by using semi-transparent color stains that allow the natural grain of the wood to show through. You can give floors and traditional wooden furniture soft, pastel tints or use brighter coordinating colors to make patchwork effects or striped designs on smaller wooden items.

Staining wood floors

An expanse of wood floor provides a canvas for original designs and color use. Floorboards can be stained in stripes and plain wood panels can be transformed with a patchwork of pastel stains.

If the wood is in poor condition, or you have concrete floors, cover the existing floor with plywood squares, mosaic panels or strip flooring. These can then be stained.

Staining furniture

Traditional wood furniture is brought to life by staining. Even old pine furniture that has been stripped can benefit from the addition of a golden stain to bring back its warmth. New pine can be stained to blend with old doors and baseboards, and existing pine furniture.

Baseboards and doors

Use a pastel-colored translucent stain to match baseboards and doors to walls that are painted or papered in soft colors. Alternatively, harmonize the decor of a room by staining floorboards, baseboards and doors in the same shade so that they will blend together beautifully.

Garden furniture

If you intend to stain furniture that remains outdoors it is important to choose a stain, varnish or sealer designed for outdoor use. Microporous stains that contain a fungicide to protect the finish against mold

▽ *Floorboards can be painted in stripes, or you can create tonal effect by staining sections of floor with pastel or primary stains.*

△ *Traditional wooden furniture can be given a new lease on life by staining. Prepare the surface by removing any existing paint or varnish finish and sanding the surface to remove any marks or scratches in the wood. Try using a stain with a faint hint of color to add a warm natural glow to the item of furniture.*

growth and an ultra-violet filter that acts against bleaching by the sun are ideal for garden furniture. This finish will be quite flat. If you want a high shine to your furniture apply a varnish designed for outdoor use over the wood stain.

Materials and equipment

Apart from the stain itself you need surprisingly little equipment to stain

wood. Buy some sandpaper to prepare the surface of the wood before you start work. A good quality brush or clean cloth is also essential so that you can apply the stain, and you may need a thinner to thin down the stain you decide to use.

Stains

Wood stains fall into two main types – those that stain the wood but give no protection to the surface, and those that are mixed with varnish so that the wood is both colored and protected at the same time.

Stain on its own This type of stain does not give any protection to the wood, so the surface will need protection by polish or oil. It is therefore especially suitable for renovating old furniture. The stain can be thinned using turpentine for oil-based stains or water for water-based stains.

This type of stain dries quickly which can make it difficult to apply evenly. Working along the grain, apply the stain sparingly with a cloth. Do not go over an area that has already been covered with stain or the finish will become blotchy. When the finish is dry, oil or polish it.

Varnish stain This type of stain colors and protects the wood at the same time. Each coat of varnish slightly deepens the color. Apply a number of layers of stain for a deep color. If you want more protection but no greater depth of color, finish off with a clear varnish instead.

Varnish stains can be polyurethane or acrylic water-based. Polyurethane varnish is available in a satin or gloss finish, and will need to be thinned with turpentine. Leave up to 12 hours drying time between coats. Acrylic-based varnish is available only in a satin finish and must be thinned before use with water. A coat of acrylic varnish takes only 30 minutes to dry and can be re-coated in two hours.

All-in-one wood stain and protective finish is also available. This is oil-based and it dries quickly. This means it can be re-coated in two hours time. It is available in a gloss or satin finish. Some brands are sold in a tester size so you can try out the color.

Colorful wood finishes Unlike opaque paint, semi-translucent colored finishes still allow the grain of the wood to show through. They are oil-based and are brushed on to give a protective flat finish. You can choose from pastel shades or more vibrant colors. If a gloss finish is required, clear varnish can be used on top of the stain.

Brushes Choose a good quality brush and use it only for varnishing. Dislodge any loose bristles before starting work, and clean the brush well after use so that it can be used again for the next project.

Cloth On curved and molded wood it is easier to achieve an even finish with a cloth than with a brush. For this method use a cloth which is soft, clean and lint free.

Preparing the wood

Wood that is to be stained needs careful preparation beforehand as any irregularities, marks or stains will be obvious once the wood stain is applied. Previously untreated, lightly colored wood shows off color best, but older surfaces can come up well if they are prepared properly.

Remove all paint or varnish from wood before applying wood stain. Fill any holes, dents and scratches with wood filler and sand the surface down to ensure a smooth finish. For sanding floors rent a large commercial sander and a smaller edging sander. Seal any bleeding knots in the wood with stain killing sealer-primer and seal open-grained wood with grain filler. If you want to lighten wood use a proprietary wood bleach.

This has the added advantage of removing any surface stains.

Test wood stain on a spare piece of the same wood or in a hidden area of the item to be stained before you start. You can then be certain of what the finished result will look like and make any changes necessary.

▽ *Colored wood finishes still allow the natural grain of the wood to show through. The pastel green translucent wood stain used on this chest of drawers looks very pretty and you could always try staining baseboards and doors to match. The tasselled knobs add a decorative touch.*

◁ *Here a red and green varnish has been applied to alternate floor panels with the third panel coated with a natural varnish for a pleasing contrast. By treating the panels in different colors, a strong pattern is formed.*

Staining a plant trough

Show off the decorative design of a wooden plant trough by highlighting its shape and pattern with a range of deep pastel, translucent paint stains. The color scheme you choose for the trough should complement the colors of any other surfaces around it, and you can plant flowers and shrubs to blend in with the scheme.

You will need

◇ Translucent paint stain in three colors
◇ ½in (1cm) and 1½in (3cm) painter's brushes
◇ Masking tape
◇ Thick, clear plastic sheeting double the area of the box base with an extra 2in (5cm) on all sides to allow for overlap
◇ Enough sand or small pebbles to cover the base to a depth of ¾in (2cm).

1 Sand new wood to a smooth finish, fill any holes with wood filler and apply primer-sealer to knots to prevent bleeding. On dark wood the colors will be less clear, so you may wish to lighten the wood first using a wood bleach. Remove any existing paint or varnish from old wood.

2 First surround the outer panels of the box with masking tape to avoid any of the color used for the box lining appearing on the outside. Also mask the leg edges on the outer frame where the green stained frame abuts them. Press down the tape lightly but firmly so that no stain can seep underneath.

▽ *This attractive wooden plant trough will make a welcome addition to any garden.*

3 Using the larger brush apply the green stain sparingly to the inside of the box, brushing in the direction of the wood grain. Stain the trellis areas of the outer container, using the smaller brush in the same way. Leave to dry. For a stronger color you can apply a second coat, but leave the first to dry overnight. Remove the tape before the stain is completely dry.

4 When the stain is dry, apply more masking tape along the green stained top edge of the box then stand this upside down on supports to hold it above the working surface. Mask all the green stained edges adjacent to the legs of the frame and stand this on small supports too.

5 Working with the wood grain, brush the pink stain on to the outer sides and underneath of the inner panels. Then use blue stain to coat the four legs of the outer container. Leave to dry. Recoat if necessary and remove tape.

6 When the box is completely dry, line with plastic sheeting. Cut the plastic in half and line the box so that the sheeting comes equally 2in (5cm) up all four sides. Add a ¾in (2cm) layer of grit or small pebbles to the base of the box before placing plants in their pots in position.

TIP	A TROUGH

You can make a similar, but simpler, decorative trough. Just cut wooden garden trellis to fit all four sides of a large, rectangular wooden box. Stain the box and trellis separately. When both are dry, glue the trellis in position and secure with screws. If necessary, touch up the trough with more colored stain.

A row of three or four basic, square wooden boxes – the type normally used as rustic plant containers – will also look effective when stained. Use a selection of pastel colors to create a harmonious combination.

Glazing

*The paint effect known as glazing
involves using glaze and paint to tone and merge
colors on a surface. The glaze is designed to
remain wet and workable long enough to enable you to apply
the color and create decorative finishes.*

△ *A green and mustard glaze was applied to the
off-white base coat of this shelf. The samples show
some other possible color effects.*

Glazing is a quick and easy paint technique which mixes wet paint and oil glaze over a dry base color. Oil glaze, then oil paint, is brushed onto a surface. While it is still wet, some of the paint and glaze mixture is wiped away with a clean, soft, lint-free cloth. The colors are then blended and toned to achieve the desired effect.

The important thing to remember with this technique is that you must work quickly, before the oil glaze becomes too dry.

Adding highlights

Glazing works especially well on furniture with ornamental details. It can be used to highlight certain areas and add shadows to others.

This paint technique can also be used to add shape and dimension to large, flat surfaces. This is done by using two different shades of the base coat – one slightly lighter and one slightly darker. Use the darker shade in the corners and edges furthest away from the light source and the lighter shade in the center and edges closest to light.

Preparation

Whatever item you choose to paint must be prepared before decorating. Glazing accentuates cracks and crevices, so make sure you do only those surface marks you want to focus on. Remove peeling or flaking paint and fill in cracks and surface flaws. Then sand and prime with an appropriate oil-based primer.

Apply two coats of the base color, lightly sanding between each coat. Use an oil-based paint. Once the second coat is dry, lightly sand and wipe with a damp cloth.

You will need

◇ Oil-based primer
◇ Oil-based base coat, flat finish (we used an off-white color)
◇ Transparent oil glaze
◇ Household oil-based paint (we used blue-green and mustard)
◇ Three 1in (2.5cm) or 2in (5cm) natural bristled paint brushes (one for the glaze and one for each paint color to be blended)
◇ Lots of soft, lint-free rags (cheesecloth or mutton cloth)
◇ Turpentine
◇ Sandpaper

Method

1 Prepare and prime the surface. Apply two coats of the base color. (See 'Preparation').

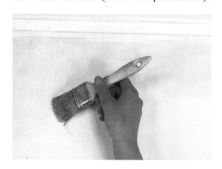

2 Liberally apply the oil glaze to the base coat. Work on just a small area at a time to enable you to apply the color and wipe it away before the glaze dries. (The glaze remains wet and workable for about 20 minutes).

3 Brush the oil-based paint on top of the glaze. Apply the blue-green color to the shadows and recesses in the molding. Add the mustard color to the flat surface and to the relief areas of the molding. Apply the paint as broadly or as gently as you like, but make sure you leave some of the base coat showing.

4 Wipe off some of the paint and glaze with a rag to reveal more of the base coat and blend and soften the colors. Whenever the cloth becomes clogged with paint and glaze, replace with a fresh cloth. Soften the surface more, either by dabbing with a soft cloth or by stippling with a natural bristled brush.

5 Once you have achieved the desired effect, allow the surface to dry and then protect it with an oil-based varnish.

Distressing

*The paint technique of distressing involves
lightly dry-brushing four to six varying shades of the
same color onto a surface. This method allows
tiny flecks of the different shades to show through,
creating a soft, mottled appearance.*

Distressing is an excellent paint technique for giving newly painted pieces of furniture, walls and doors the mellow appearance of age. This fairly easy technique can be used to match new furniture to older items, or simply for the pleasure of the striking, yet subtle, textured effect which can be achieved.

Preparation

Furniture needs to be properly prepared and primed. When distressing interior walls, it is best to work directly on the primed plaster, as this will enhance the texture of the paint effect. Walls painted in warm earth tones, such as yellow ochre or burnt sienna, take on the appearance of a fresco.

For interior walls

Scrape away loose, chipped paint and fill and sand any surface imperfections and cracks. Raw plaster should be primed with a water-based primer. Make sure that previously painted walls are completely dust free and clean before you work on them.

◁ *Tones of one color are layered, starting with lightest tone.*

▽ *These stencilled details were added after the third layer of paint had been applied.*

For furniture

Items of furniture should be prepared following the instructions in the previous Glazing chapter, but using a water-based undercoat or primer rather than an oil-based one. While major surface cracks and flaws should be filled, minor imperfections add to the textured effect of this paint technique. Use your judgement to decide which to fill and which to leave as character. For more information, see pages 47-48.

Paint mixing

For a successful finish, various shades of one color need to be mixed separately. To do this, pour small amounts of white latex into individual containers; then add varying amounts of the chosen color to each and stir well to give four to six different shades of color. If the shades look too similar, add more white or more of the chosen color.

Small amounts of a different color can be added to one or two of the shades to tint them slightly further. Raw or burnt umber 'age' a shade while brighter colors, such as yellow or orange, add a lively hue. Do not be afraid to experiment with one of the shades, as the layering method only allows flecks of each color to show through.

Distressing

You will need

◇ White, water-based latex paint to act as the base for mixing the different shades
◇ Water-based latex paint in the color of your choice
◇ 1-2in (2.5-5cm) painter's brush for painting furniture or 3-4in (7.5-10cm) painter's brush for painting walls
◇ 4-6 containers for mixing the various tints or shades used for the distressing
◇ Newspaper
◇ Fine grade abrasive paper

Method

1 Prepare and prime the surface. Mix the paints, as described opposite in 'Paint mixing'.

2 Using the lightest shade, paint a base coat over the entire primed surface. Leave it to dry thoroughly and then gently sand with fine grade abrasive paper, so that a little of the primed surface shows through. Wipe away the dust with a slightly damp cloth.

4 At this point the surface might look blotchy, but do not worry as the overall effect is achieved by building up a number of layers. Continue working, lightly and dryly, from light to dark paint, allowing flecks of previously painted colors to show through. Allow each color to dry before proceeding to the next.

3 Working from the lightest shade to the darkest, take the next shade in the sequence and apply it, lightly and dryly. To do this, dip the brush into the paint and remove the excess paint by brushing onto a piece of newspaper. Do not allow your brush to become heavily laden with paint. Start painting, varying the direction of your brush stroke, from side to side and up and down. The idea is that you do not completely cover the base coat, allowing spots and patches of the previous coat to show through. Leave each coat of paint to dry before applying the next layer.

5 As you apply your third and fourth colors the brush strokes will disappear and the effect will start to look soft and mottled. The successive layers of paint build up an interesting texture which you can actually feel. Continue adding layers of paint until you have worked your way through all of the colors. When finished, leave to dry completely.

Finishing off

It is not essential to seal walls after they have been distressed. If necessary, they can be kept clean by gently and carefully washing them with warm soapy water. Major marks or scratches can be quickly touched up by distressing over them.

Furniture can be protected with two coats of matt or semi-gloss polyurethane varnish. However, it is not necessary to varnish the items: as with the walls, areas can be touched up by distressing over them; alternatively, for a more distressed, aged look, worn areas can be left as they are.

TIP	DECORATIVE FEATURES

For a more authentic look, extra decorative features, such as the stencilled design on the washstand door in this chapter, should be added before applying the last distressed layer.

Creating an aged look

These effects can be taken a step further, to achieve a more antique look. This involves applying layers of paint or varnish and gently sanding between the layers to remove some of the color.

Some people go to even greater lengths to give furniture an authentically aged look. Keys, chains and even bricks can be bashed against or dropped onto areas of the furniture to give an appearance of general wear and tear. But this must be done very subtly, as it is easy to overdo it: look at genuinely old items to see which parts have been naturally worn, such as handles, or corners of drawers or table tops which people have handled over many years.

If further decorative details are to be applied, these should also be given a look of age. New gilding can be made dull by coating it with a solution of burnt umber gouache mixed with a little water and a drop of detergent. Decorative lining or stencilled designs can be gently rubbed away in places to make them more in keeping with the piece.

△ *This new cabinet was given a distressed paint effect to make it look like a period piece*

◁ *Small repairs were carried out on this old blanket box, then its age was enhanced with distressing.*

◁ *A Tyrolean painted coffer, dated 1800, shows the true beauty of a paint effect that has mellowed and worn with time. It is just this type of effect that the modern distressed paint techniques aim to emulate.*

Marbling

The rich effect of marble is surprisingly easy to imitate.
By using the appropriate type of paint and the right equipment,
you can create small panels of marble to decorate
accessories or furniture, or even use the technique to
cover larger areas, such as doors or walls.

The fantasy effect

Marble is a luxurious material, rarely used in its natural form these days except for small areas – tiles, fireplaces and accessories such as boxes and lamp bases are the most common examples. In history, it was used more extravagantly in grand households, for floors and even walls. It is an expensive material and difficult to handle, so it makes sense to have a bit of fun and develop your color skills to imitate the effect.

Surfaces for marbling

For a true-to-life effect, apply the finish to the type of surface where you might find the real thing: wooden boxes, fireplace mantels, beneath a chair rail, or even a panelled door. Wooden floors – stripped floorboards, floors levelled with particle board or plywood, or prepared concrete floors – can look particularly effective with a marbled finish, especially if they are painted to imitate tiles. However, they will need extra protection over the paint to prevent rapid wear.

Try to reproduce a natural effect by observing marble as it is actually used: the size of panels of marble is limited because of the weight of the material. It is unusual to find large panels – large areas are usually clad in several smaller panels, often arranged to create a pattern. The weight also affects where it is used. Permanent fixtures, for example, baseboards, are realistic situations for marble. Marble doors or windows would be impossibly heavy, but if it is a fantasy effect you are after, the paint finish is a practical option.

Color and tone

Look at the natural variations of color and the veining effect in real marble. You will find examples on existing fireplaces, and in particular as a facing material on commercial buildings.

Materials and equipment

Paints

Ordinary household paints cannot be used on their own to create a marbled paint effect. There are some special materials which you will need.

Translucent glaze is an oil-based, translucent paint medium, rather like varnish. It is used for many paint effects, because it has what is known as 'a long open time'. This means that it takes a long time to dry, so you can work it, adding color which sinks into the surface, without bleeding into it. The glaze has no pigment, so that even if you add color (in the form of oil-based household or artist's paints), successive coats have a translucence, allowing base colors to show through.

Household paints are used for the base coat and also to tint the glaze. Use only oil-based paints (in the form of gloss and semi-gloss paint) which will mix with the translucent

Artist's oil paints

Lint-free rag

Universal stainers

Household paint brush

Badger hair brush

Round brush

Feathers

Translucent glaze

Sponge

Artist's brushes

In most types of marble, an all-over mottled effect is interrupted by veins and variations in the density or tone of color. The effect is imitated by mixing carefully graduated tones of paint and building up a base color. While this coat is still wet, the 'veins' in another color are added. Before the paint dries, the whole effect can be softened by brushing over the surface.

The natural luster of marble is only evident when the stone is cut and polished. When painting imitation marble, this polish is created by adding coats of glaze, rather like varnish, so that the color sinks beneath the surface.

glaze. The colors you use will depend on the marble you are trying to imitate – creamy whites, palest greys, or rich dark greens, even pinks and reds.

Universal stainers can be used to tint the base coat, or to create subtle variations in tone. They can also be used to tint the glaze and are particularly effective when you want to add color without detracting from its translucence, in order to build up the 'polish' of marble.

Artist's oil paints can also be used to tint both the base coat and subsequent glaze coats. However, their main use is to paint in veins of color. Traditional shades to use are burnt sienna and dark grey on pale marble; white and green on black backgrounds, and so on. It is always worth having some white paint on hand to add body to colors and for extra emphasis when painting in veins.

Turpentine is used to thin the coats of color. Suggested proportions for mixing are given on the following page. Mixing turpentine with artist's oil paint before adding it to paint or glaze makes it easier to blend.

Brushes

Household paint brushes should be of good quality. Use clean brushes, which are free of dust and do not shed hairs. The size depends on the surface you are painting: for small items, a ½in brush may be adequate; for walls or floors you will need a 4in brush for the main part of the surface and a 1in brush for corners that are difficult to get to.

Artist's brushes are used for painting in details. Stiff, round brushes are useful for stippling background color. Softer, broad brushes can be used to add variations in tone, and soft, fine brushes are best for adding veins. Build up a collection of brushes, and experiment with the different effects they give.

Feathers are often used by professionals for softening the veins – or even for painting them in. If you are tackling a large area, make sure you have several feathers of similar weight, as they tend to get clogged with paint and are easily damaged.

Sponges and rags can be used at various stages in the work to create mottled patterns.

Clean soft brushes can also be used to soften the effect. Professional decorators use long soft brushes of badger hair, but you can also use large artists' brushes or even make-up brushes as long as they do not shed hairs.

△ *With every layer of glaze, veins and mottling that you add, so the surface you are decorating takes on the cool distinction of marble. The pale marble effect that has been applied to this mirror and plinth gives them a new distinction that is easy to imitate.*

TIP BRUSH CARE

Always use good-quality brushes and clean them thoroughly in turpentine, oil thinners or brush cleaner after use. Store them with handles down, so there is no pressure on the bristles. Before use, always flick your thumb across the bristles of the brush, to get rid of dust and check for loose bristles. If the brush starts to shed hairs, discard it immediately.

Applying the colors

In order to create individual colors and a workable medium, it is always necessary to experiment before tackling a job. The type of surface you are painting, the brushes and equipment you use and the brand of paint you buy are all part of the finished effect – even the weather can affect the outcome.

Start with a well-prepared surface, free from splinters or flaking paint. Seal with primer if it is porous. You must start with an evenly absorbent surface.

Choose and mix a color for the base coat – you can usually use a standard household paint. The undercoat may be sufficient.

For the next coat, mix a glaze. This may be tinted with any of the types of paint described on the previous pages – add household oil paint for a more opaque color, or just universal stainers if you want the color beneath to show through.

Adding texture and tone

After applying the glaze, work in variations of tone to the background color, by dabbing on artist's oil paint or tinted oil based paint. Use brushes, sponges – even rags – to break up the color of the base coat.

Next, add a structure of veins across the surface, using an artist's paint brush. Again, you can use artist's oils or tints of oil paint, with or without glaze. While the paint is still wet, soften the lines as necessary, using a feather or soft brush. When doing this, always work in one direction, to keep a hard edge along one side of the veins and a faded effect along the other.

You can build up variations in tone and add extra depth to the surface by adding further coats of glaze, mixed fairly thin and lightly tinted with color. As you build up successive coats, the veins will sink beneath the surface.

Mixing glazes

For an opaque glaze, good proportions to work with are three parts oil-based glaze, five parts off-white oil paint and two parts turpentine. Mix the paint with the glaze, then add the turpentine to give a creamy consistency.

For a more translucent glaze, tint the glaze with oil paints or stainers, then add a roughly equal quantity of turpentine.

Pale marbling effect

You can create many interesting tonal effects using pale colors. Here varying shades of grey have been used, a hint of umber adds a realistic finishing touch.

You will need

◇ Primer or oil-based paint (dependent on surface)
◇ Artist's oil paints in umber and varying shades of grey
◇ Translucent glaze
◇ Household paint brushes
◇ Soft, flat artists' brush
◇ Soft make-up brush
◇ Natural sponge
◇ Lint-free rags
◇ Very fine sandpaper
◇ Turpentine

1 Sand the surface to be decorated and apply primer (on wood or metal) or oil (on walls) in a suitable color. The paint effect will look better if you take care over this stage.

2 If necessary, apply a further coat to act as a base coat for the decorative finish. Tint it slightly with grey oil paint, and use a sponge to create lightly mottled areas.

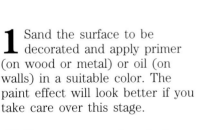

3 Using mid-grey artists' oil and an artists' brush, start to create a random trellis of diagonal veins across the surface.

4 Strengthen some of the veins with darker colors, then soften the effect by brushing over the surface with a soft brush.

5 Use a natural sponge to create variations in tone, lifting off color or applying extra color where needed.

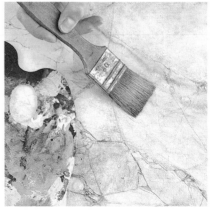

6 Apply a translucent glaze, with a light umber tint. In some patches, add extra coats of glaze for a natural effect.

Bambooing

*Imitating the natural look of bamboo brings
a stylish feel to previously uninspiring furniture. By
taking the technique one step further, and using
colors from your imagination, the fantasy effect created can range
from the sophisticated to the surreal.*

Unlike paint effects such as sponging and rag-rolling, which bring texture and interest to decorations and furniture, fantasy effects create something altogether different. They take a surface or object and change our perception of it. A plain, wooden floor can take on the grandiose feel of marble; a dull picture frame is given the luxury of tortoiseshell; an uninspiring room is made to look quite grand with antiquing and gilding.

Bambooing, despite being fairly intricate, is perhaps the easiest fantasy effect to undertake, adding individuality to tired furnishings.

▽ *This staircase reflects the interest in oriental styles.*

What is bambooing?

Bambooing was developed in the eighteenth century in response to the passion in Europe for all things oriental.

Bambooing is a fine technique that can use natural colors to imitate the look of real bamboo or artificial colors for an unreal fantasy effect. The bands and knots of natural bamboo are reproduced, usually in unrealistic colors. It is most convincing when used on light pieces of furniture such as chairs, tables and plant stands.

Bamboo effects can be applied to normal wood, although plaster of Paris may be used to alter the shape of the wood for even greater authenticity. The best 'unreal' effects are achieved on pieces of furniture made from natural bamboo. During the height of its popularity, the technique was applied to furnishings and fittings carved or cast to look like bamboo.

▽ *The shapes, sizes and details of real bamboo provide a fine natural example of how anything goes when creating a bamboo effect.*

The look of bamboo

The actual detail of the bamboo can be added in various ways. The idea is to aim for bands of graduated color at each of the ring-joints of the bamboo (you will have to decide where to position these if you are not using natural bamboo or bamboo-turned wood). Running down the length of the bamboo, tapering V-shapes from the ring-joints are painted to represent the spines of the bamboo, while small knots or 'eyes' are randomly dotted over the surface of the wood, fairly close to the spines.

Materials and equipment

Paints

Base coat This must have a flat finish, and be oil-based for durability. You can simply use several layers of primer for the base coat or, for the best results, finish the undercoat with an oil-based paint.

Top coat Traditionally, oil-based glaze was used, mixed with oil paint to give a certain opacity, and tinted with artist's oil paints or universal stainers. More paint was added to create progressively darker and more opaque mixtures for the bamboo details.

It is not essential to use the traditional glaze to create the effect, as artist's oils mixed with varnish produce a similar result. However, the most convenient paints to use are artist's acrylics, thinned with water. It is much easier to achieve fantasy effects with these colors, which have the advantage of being quick drying, so you can paint the shades in a matter of hours.

Varnish

Whatever paint you use it is necessary to give the item two or three coats of polyurethane varnish to protect against accidental damage and wear and tear. Low sheen varnish is better for paler tones, but if you use oriental blacks, jades and golds you will need a gloss varnish to create a lacquered effect.

Brushes

Regular decorators' paint brushes or flat, soft-bristled artists' brushes can be used for the base coat and the bamboo effect bands. You will need a clean brush for varnishing. The greater detail of the rings, spines and eyes requires a number 1 and finer brushes.

The bamboo shape

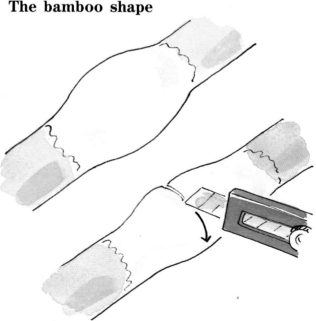

To enhance the fantasy effect it is possible to add shape to a plain piece of wood by using plaster of Paris. Make up a fairly liquid plaster of Paris mixture and use your finger to apply a little to the wood at the point where you ring to be. This can be rather tedious, but the plaster dries quickly so you can build up the ridge using several layers. Then carve the plaster with a craft knife and rub down with fine sandpaper. Prime both the plaster and wood prior to decoration.

Preparing the surface

If you are using bamboo that has not been decorated before but has been polished, rub down with fine steel wool and denatured alcohol. This is particularly important with wax polish, which will prevent the paint from adhering. Rub down previously painted items with fine sandpaper.

Prime any bare wood so that it is ready to take a coat of paint. Alternatively you can use a dual purpose primer/undercoat. Ensure that you have all the right brushes on hand. You will need a small container in which to mix your colors.

1 Apply at least three layers of base coat, rubbing down well between coats: for a particularly fine, smooth finish, rub down with wet-and-dry abrasive paper that has been dipped in soapy water. If you have decided to use oil-based paint for the top layer of the base coat, allow the paint to dry and then rub down lightly to reduce the sheen.

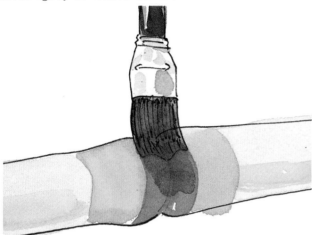

2 If you are not using natural bamboo, decide on the positions for the rings and mark the center of each ring in pencil. The rings are usually about 6in apart and can be evenly or unevenly spaced. Using a pale acrylic paint and a ⅝in brush, paint a 2in band around the bamboo. Repeat until all the rings are complete, and allow to dry.

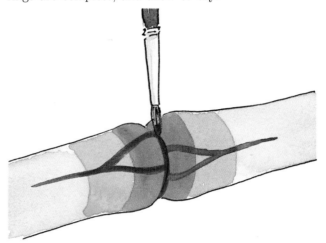

3 Using a slightly darker and less translucent paint mixture, add a second band of color inside the first about ⅝in wide. Even when working on a straight surface, the combination of this and the lighter band creates a contoured appearance. Repeat for each band and allow to dry.

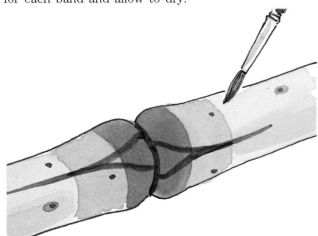

4 Using the darkest tone of paint, pick out the notch line around the ring of the bamboo with a number 1 artists' brush. At the same time, using the same tone but a number 00 artists' brush, pick out fine V-shaped spines running from the rings along a third of the length of the individual bamboo section.

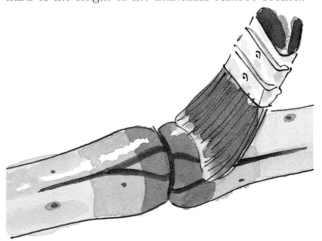

5 Plan the position of the 'eyes' carefully – one or two fairly close to each spine will be plenty. Using the artists' brushes, apply a blob of pale or mid-tone paint followed by a tiny dot in the center and two or three further dots in the darkest tone.

6 When you are happy with the effect and the paint is completely dry, apply at least three coats of either silk or gloss polyurethane protective varnish, depending on the finish you wish to create. Rub down lightly with fine sandpaper between coats.

DESIGN LIBRARY

The colors you choose for the bamboo effect depend on the overall effect desired, and the decor of the room. For a natural bamboo look choose pale yellow ochre or sienna for the base coat, adding rings and eyes in tones of amber and umber.

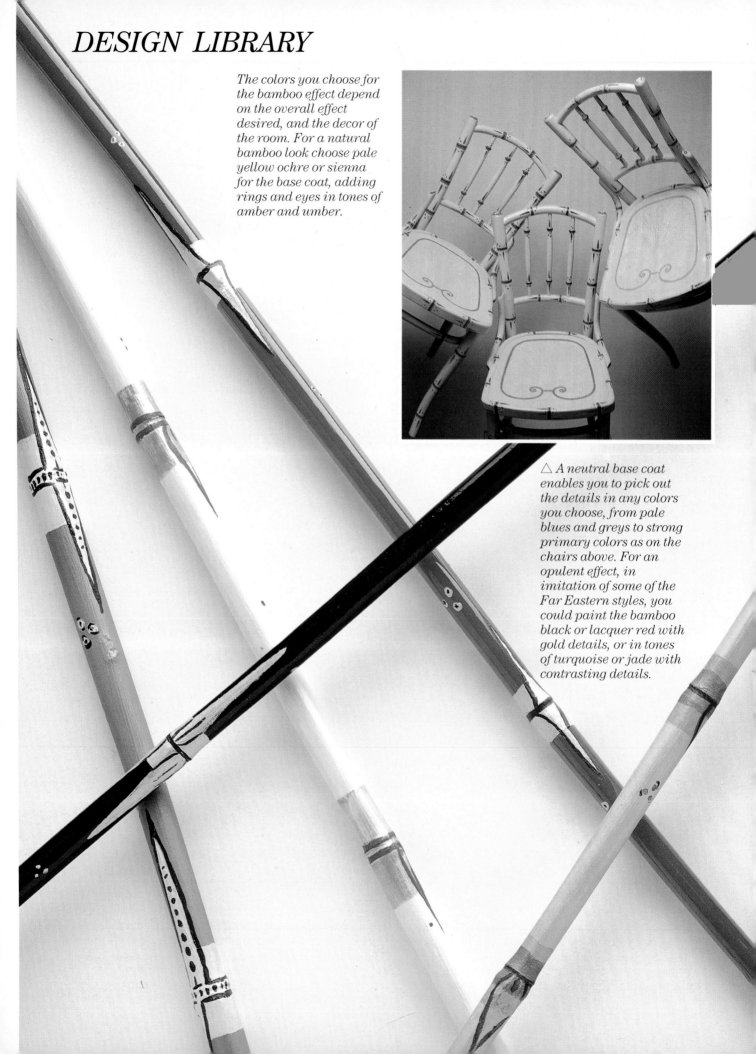

△ *A neutral base coat enables you to pick out the details in any colors you choose, from pale blues and greys to strong primary colors as on the chairs above. For an opulent effect, in imitation of some of the Far Eastern styles, you could paint the bamboo black or lacquer red with gold details, or in tones of turquoise or jade with contrasting details.*

Tortoiseshelling

*For thousands of years the beautiful translucent shell
of the hawksbill sea turtle provided a rich adornment – for a
price. Now, despite the trade ban on 'tortoiseshell', you can still
capture its unique attraction by the careful application
of straightforward painting techniques.*

Like many fantasy paint techniques, tortoiseshelling was developed to provide an inexpensive
substitute for a much sought after
commodity. Real tortoiseshell has
always been a rare and precious
adornment – even before the current concern for animal welfare.

In 1973 the hawksbill sea turtle
– source of the much coveted 'tortoiseshell' – was declared an en-
dangered species and a world trade
ban was issued.

However, the attraction of the
shell, with its distinctive brown and
black markings, and beige, tawny

and blond shades – even reds –
remains unforgettable.

The scarcity of the raw material
has tended to limit its use to
smaller items such as on hair
brushes, picture frames and trays,
or for use as inlay on furniture.

The fake paint method does not

have this limitation but is nevertheless best used on small objects where it produces the quickest and most authentic results. The finish is time consuming – worth considering before embarking on a major project such as a table top.

Tortoiseshelling can also be worked in bright color combinations – blue and green for example – or can be combined with a plain marble or simulated ivory finish, but don't go over the top.

▽ *An Antwerp tortoiseshell and ebony veneered cabinet on a stand dating from the third quarter of the 17th Century. A plain cabinet at home could be 'dressed' with the tortoiseshell look.*

The look of tortoiseshell
It is a good idea to keep a piece of real tortoiseshell or a picture of it by you as you work, but try to capture the essence of tortoiseshell rather than aim for a photographic representation of the natural markings which may look labored.

The markings are created by applying tinted glaze in oval-shaped patches on to a paler background. The pattern should run diagonally across the work – preferably a flat or slightly curved surface – with

bands of color diverging slightly. Work in a diagonal direction when building up the pattern. Blend in the glaze at the edges to imitate the graduations in color which occur in real tortoiseshell. The darkest tone should be at the center of the markings, fading to rich chestnut and golden brown at the edges.

Materials and equipment
Paints
Remember you will not need huge amounts of paint if you are working on small items.

Base coat Use two coats on an oil-based paint with a semi-gloss or similar soft sheen finish. Gloss paint is too shiny for tortoiseshelling. The colors used depend on the final coloring you want to achieve; the base coat is usually quite a strong chrome or acid yellow. Bare wood needs sealing first with a primer/undercoat product.

Top coat For a realistic tortoiseshell effect, make the first layer from 70 per cent glaze, 20 percent turpentine and 10 per cent artists' oil in raw sienna. The markings are made by tinting the glaze with artists' oils in progressively darker shades of burnt umber and black.

Varnish
Clear polyurethane varnish is essential to protect the finish. Decorative items need only two coats of varnish but anything subject to wear (such as a table or tray) should be given three coats. Choose a mid-sheen varnish for a natural look. Varnish dries quickly so it is essential to work fast. For this reason, don't work on too large an area at once. If you intend to cover a large area, work in alternate panels, leaving each to dry before tackling the next.

Brushes
For the best results use specialist brushes. You need an ordinary paint brush for applying the base coat, an artists' 'fitch' for the glaze, a softening brush for blending and a small stencil brush for spattering. A piece of lint free cloth is also needed for softening the surface of the glaze to give a more natural-looking finished result.

Preparing the surface

Strip the piece clean of any polish using turpentine and steel wool followed by detergent solution. Metal or wood items must be sanded down (wood should be sanded along the grain). Treat bare wood with a coat of primer/sealer. For metal, use an appropriate primer followed by undercoat.

1 Apply two coats of light colored oil paint, sanding lightly between each coat, then wiping clean to give a fine finish. Work diagonally throughout.

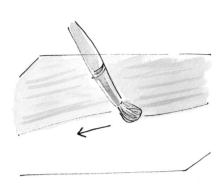

2 Apply a coat of glaze with the fitch, working back and forth to create a dragged effect.

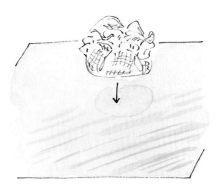

3 Still working diagonally, soften the lines by dabbing the glaze with a lint free cloth.

4 To create the characteristic tortoiseshell markings, add more raw sienna to the glaze to darken it and apply with the fitch in oval-shaped patches about 2-3 inches long. Keep the outline random, overlapping it from time to time.

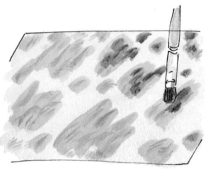

5 Add burnt umber to the mix to darken it again and make further marks inside the patches. Then add more burnt umber and a touch of black for the darkest markings and apply in the center of the previous burnt umber marks.

6 Blur the outlines with a softening brush, working the colors in well so that they merge into each other. Finish by blending away any remaining hard outlines with a random movement of the brush. If the glaze is still wet you can repeat this process to give an even more realistic effect.

7 Spatter tiny dots of the darkest glaze over the surface using a small stencil brush. Dip no more than one-third of the bristle length into the paint. Tap the base of the handle against a straight edge held over the work and aim to create a fine shower of paint.

8 If you want to break up the pattern you can spatter turpentine on the surface while it is still wet, giving an antique effect. Load an artists' brush with turpentine and tap it against a stick held over the surface of the work. It takes a few seconds for the effect to become noticeable. Tap lightly and leave for half a minute

9 Allow the glaze to dry and then apply polyurethane varnish for protection. Rub this down with fine sandpaper and clean between coats. Several coats of varnish create a deep, protective sheen, enhancing the effect.

△ *In this traditional style reception room the decor has been given the tortoiseshelling treatment, with the painting technique applied to the door frames and the cornice.*

Colors

Natural tortoiseshell has a beauty of its own but the design also lends itself to other deep, rich colors. Try blending green and dark blue on a sea colored background, or combine ruby red with dark brown for a sophisticated effect.

For a successful finish, simply remember to keep to related colors, choosing a pale tone for the background and building up the markings with increasingly saturated shades so that the darkest shade is in the center. The darkest shade is also used for the drops, which are spattered lightly over the surface for a naturalistic effect.

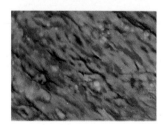

△ *Here are three entirely different looks created by using the same 'tortoiseshelling' techniques. The bottom two examples use different color combinations from the traditional browns.*

Porphyry

Although porphyry rock is neither rare nor expensive, it is an easy and popular stone to recreate successfully using paints. Its natural grainy appearance is imitated by spattering varying tones of a chosen color over a solid base color.

What is porphyry?

Porphyry is an igneous rock with a grainy appearance. Highly polished, and hard and cool to the touch, it is similar to marble, except that it has few or no veins. Although it is usually reddish purple, porphyry does occur in a range of other colors including green or violet; reddish orange; and brown, veined with quartz and speckled with pink, red and green. Some types of porphyry also contain tiny speckles of iron (fool's gold).

Real porphyry is used mainly to make small objects, such as table and desk tops, decorative inlays and ornamental bases for stands. For an impressive paint effect, try copying the appearance of this stone to decorate boxes, plain lamp bases and other small items of furniture.

Creating the effect

The best results are achieved by imitating the natural colors of real porphyry. A porphyry finish is created by spattering the base color with three or more tones of the same colors.

The spattering should be dense enough to cover most of the base color. The spatter effect can be made finer or coarser by tapping closer and farther away from the surface; alternatively, for larger spatters, thin the paint mixture with turpentine. Glaze is used for the base color but it should not be added to the spatter mixture, as it will produce a lumpy, uneven finish.

Materials and equipment

Artists' oil colors in three toning shades, a transparent glaze and turpentine are needed for painting this finish, plus a range of good quality brushes and a chamois cloth.

You will need

◇ Artists' oils: alizarin crimson, burnt sienna, burnt umber and titanium white
◇ Transparent oil glaze
◇ Turpentine (to thin the glaze slightly)
◇ Large fitch and small fitch
◇ Chamois cloth
◇ Badger hair softening brush
◇ Gloss varnish
◇ Paint tray

Method

1 If necessary, prepare the surface by sanding any rough areas with sandpaper and then priming.

2 Make a deep, reddish purple colored glaze by mixing the ingredients together in the following proportions: 45 per cent alizarin crimson; 30 per cent burnt sienna; 10 per cent burnt umber; 10 per cent glaze and 5 per cent turpentine. Using the large fitch, apply it thinly and evenly to the surface; try to produce varying tones of color.

3 Bunch the chamois cloth into a pad in your hand and gently pat the glazed surface to remove any brush strokes and surplus paint.

4 To remove any remaining marks, lightly touch over the surface with the softening brush, taking care not to add any more brush marks.

5 Mix the artists' oils separately with a little turpentine to make red, dusky pink and red-brown color (if necessary, add a little titanium white).

6 Dip the small fitch in one of the mixtures and then wipe it against the side of the paint tray to test the consistency of the paint. For spattering, the paint should be quite runny.

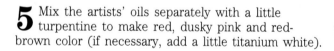

7 To spatter the paint finely, hold the fitch in one hand and drag the index finger of the other hand through the bristle tips – remember that the thicker the mixture is, the smaller the spatters will be. If you want bigger blobs, thin the mixture first with turpentine.

8 Repeat the spattering technique with the other two colors.

9 Leave to dry overnight. Then, for a polished finish, cover with two coats of gloss varnish.

The art of stencilling

*In a world dominated by mass-produced designs
and patterns, the simple technique of painting color through a
decorative cut-out shape enables you to create
your own beautiful designs and color schemes, and to experiment
and to express yourself in your own home.*

Stencilling is infinitely versatile. It can be used to make patterns or to create large, bold effects; it can produce a single motif or a border design; and it can be used to decorate walls, furniture and lampshades. It is the perfect way to produce tailor-made and coordinated decorations that are also individual.

The materials and techniques for stencilling on surfaces such as plaster, paint, wood and metal are described on the following pages. You can create interesting effects on textures such as basketwork and cane furniture. Many different weights and finishes of fabric can also be successfully stencilled, from plain closely woven cottons to textured cloths and sheers. Stencilling on fabric is covered on pages 77-82.

Surfaces should be clean, sound and preferably smooth. If you wish to stencil on natural wood, for example, floors or furniture, you can work directly on to the surface. Try a small area to see if the color 'bleeds' along the grain. If it does, seal it first with a coat of clear matt varnish. It is essential to remove any old varnish or polish before starting (the new paint will not adhere permanently to a glossy varnish or a waxy surface).

Materials and equipment

Paints

Whichever type of paint you use, you will need only a small amount; a small tube or can should be sufficient.

Water-based paints are fast-drying, enabling you to work quickly without smudging the work. Latex paints come in a wide color range, and can be tinted with acrylic paints.

Artist's acrylic paints come in a wide range of colors and can also be mixed together to create the exact shade you want. They are stocked by most art shops.

Oil-based paints Flat or semi-gloss paint is durable and effective but takes longer to dry than a water-based paint.

Other paints Water- and oil-based stencil crayons are available from specialist shops. When using oil-based crayons, rub on to an uncut area of the stencil and then use this as a 'palette' for charging the brush with paint. Metallic powders, spray paints and wood stains can also be used.

Varnish Surfaces subject to heavy wear will need sealing. Use a clear matt or gloss polyurethane varnish and apply two to four days after stencilling so that the paint has had time to dry out thoroughly.

△ *Before stencilling, the knob on this wooden drawer was taken off and the old paint removed. The wood was sealed with matt varnish. After stencilling, further coats of varnish were applied to the stencilled, re-assembled drawer for a durable finish.*

Stencils

Ready-made stencils are available in a whole range of designs from large home centers, some art and craft shops and specialist suppliers (often by mail order). You can buy stencils ready-cut or with the areas marked out for you to cut out.

Most stencils are made from waxed manila-stock paper or acetate sheet. Some stencils have a different sheet for each color and each one must be accurately positioned. Others have the whole design on one sheet if you are working with more than one color, you must block out, or mask, one area with tape while working on another.

Acetate is transparent, so you can see the other colors through it and position the stencil more accurately. Acetate does, however, have a tendency to curl.

Manila is the traditional stencilling material. It is stable to work with, but not so easy for a beginner as you cannot tell if it is lined up perfectly until you've finished applying the color.

Brushes

Stencil brushes are round with short stiff bristles which have been cut square at the end to give a soft, stippled effect. They are available in a variety of sizes. Ideally, you should buy a brush for each color and match the size of brush to the scale of the design.

It is important to clean the brushes whenever you finish working. Clean brushes in water for latex paints, and turpentine if using oil-based paint. To ensure that the bristles keep a good shape when drying, use an elastic band to hold them together. Never leave brushes bristles-down in water or turpentine as this ruins their shape.

Sponges

You can use a natural or synthetic sponge to apply paint through the stencil. Cut the sponge into small pieces and use them to dab on the color. This gives a pleasant textured look to the final design and is particularly effective over large areas of plain color.

Manila paper stencil

Acetate stencil

Paint tray

Paint

Masking tape

Brushes

Brass stencil

Natural sponge

Stencilling a single-colored motif

1 Pour some paint into a saucer. If necessary dilute it with a little water (water-based paint) or turpentine (oil-based paint). The consistency of the paint should be creamy – if it is too thin it will run and seep under the edge of the stencil.

2 Position the stencil and fix it in place with masking tape. Dip the brush into the paint and remove any excess on scrap paper.

3 Using one hand to press the stencil firmly against the surface, dab paint onto the stencil until the cut-out areas are filled.

4 Leave the paint to dry. Remove the tape and lift off the stencil. Don't slide the stencil or you'll smudge the work. Clean off the stencil when you've finished with a soft rag dipped in soapy water (for water-based paints) or turpentine (for oil-based paints). Store stencils flat when dry.

△ *A delicate green leaf design decorates this panelled door. The molding is picked out in a lighter tone of the same color. Doors lend themselves to stencilling with both borders and single motifs. Panels within doors are a natural defined space for decoration with colored motifs.*

TIP COLOR SHADING

Subtle coloring is more attractive for most subjects than solid areas of color and adds to the hand-done appeal. Use the brush fairly dry so that it makes a stippled mark rather than a solid blob. To create interest and subtle shading on single color areas build up the color in certain areas. A similar effect can be achieved with a sponge.

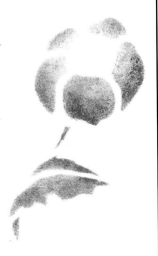

Stencilling a multi-colored motif

Using a single stencil

If the whole design is contained on a single stencil, you can complete the painting without removing the stencil. Simply mask off all but the area you are working on each time using small pieces of paper or cardboard and masking tape.

Using a series of stencils

If there is a separate stencil for each color, position and paint your first stencil and let it dry. Now plan the position of the next stencil.

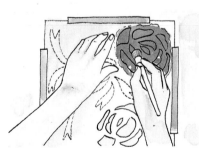

Acetate stencils are transparent so you can see the area already painted through the stencil and can therefore position the second and subsequent stencils accordingly.

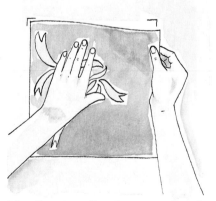

Manila stencils obscure painted areas so mark the position of the corners of the first stencil with a light pencil before removing it – these are known as registration marks. Match up the corners of subsequent stencils with these marks.

Stencilling borders

*Now that you have mastered the basics of stencilling
and experimented with individual motifs, why not try your hand
at border designs? These can be used to enhance
a room with few architectural details, or as a way of
emphasizing existing features.*

Border stencils can be used in many ways to enhance features and coordinate a look. There are numerous designs available to suit every taste and style – modern, traditional, folk or classical motifs abound.

△ *A delicate, continuous border in soft, muted colors has been used to create patterned 'panels' and accentuate the elegant window.*

Planning the design

Before you can begin stencilling you need to work out and mark the position of each motif. This is particularly important with continuous, architectural borders or for smaller borders. For freer designs or where motifs are spaced out along a wall, it is not so critical.

When stencilling on walls, bear in mind that they are rarely absolutely straight and the corners are hardly ever at true right angles. This means that you cannot use the walls as an accurate guide and, even with the most careful planning, you often need to make final adjustments by eye.

Positioning the border

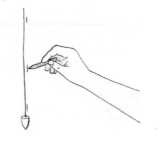

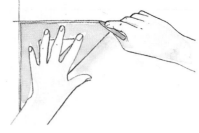

1 **Marking the vertical** Use a plumb line to find the true vertical and mark with chalk; only draw in the area to be stencilled. The chalk can be rubbed out when you have finished stencilling.

2 **Marking the horizontal** Using a set square, mark a horizontal line at right angles to the vertical one, and level with the top or bottom of your stencil. Position the stencil on this line.

Non-continuous border

This is a repeated single motif spaced evenly around a room. Take each wall separately and calculate how many times the stencil will fit into the space – the spacing between the motifs should be equal. On plain walls, work outwards from the center of each wall. If there is a feature (a chimney) placed off-center, feature and walls on either side are treated separately and the first motif centered each time.

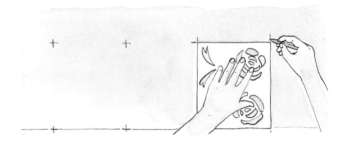

Continuous border

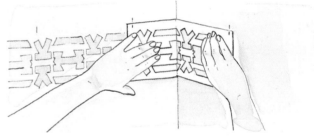

1 Some patterns are designed to be a continuous band. Keeping the border level (even if your surface is not), calculate how many times the stencil fits into the space with each motif touching – you will probably have to cheat with the last motif so start in a corner or somewhere unobtrusive.

2 To turn a corner, calculate where on the stencil the angle will occur. Place a metal ruler along this line and score it with the back of a scalpel or craft knife. For an inward angle score the back of the stencil; for an outward one, score the front. Bend the stencil over the ruler to make a smooth fold.

Mitering a corner

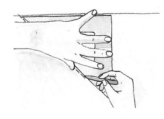

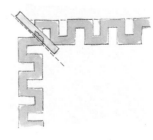

1 Mark the horizontal line as before. Using a set square, draw a line at an angle of 45° to cross it. Place masking tape along the line.

2 Stencil along the horizontal line, taking the paint over the edge of the tape. Remove tape and leave the motif until thoroughly dry.

3 Reposition the tape along the other side of diagonal line; over the completed work. Repeat as before. When dry, rub out the line.

Note: Do not worry too much about finding the perfect area of the stencil for the miter.

Whether stencilling a panel, around a door or window, it is almost inevitable that not all the miters will be at an ideal part of the design. You will, in fact, find that once the design is completed, any discrepancy is hardly noticeable.

Toy box

You will need

◇ Cardboard box
◇ Stencil brush or sponge
◇ Prepared stencil
◇ Latex paint for base
◇ Acrylic, stencil or latex paints for the design
◇ Masking tape

Paint the box with latex and leave to dry. Fix the stencil in position with masking tape. Cover the areas not being stencilled and apply the first color. Allow to dry and repeat with subsequent colors. For added protection coat the finished box with varnish.

A plain cardboard box is transformed into a cheerful children's toy box using our geometric stencil design.

Tracing stencils from printed designs

Stencil designs must be transferred onto a stencil sheet before cutting. The easiest way is to trace the design onto transparent acetate. With masking tape, secure the acetate in position over the design and trace along the outline of the pattern. To ensure a flowing, continuous line, hold the pen in a relaxed way. Draw straight lines with a rulers.

Cutting out the stencil

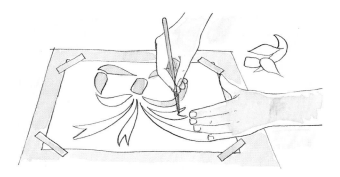

With masking tape, stick the stencil firmly to a cutting board or mat. Using a scalpel or craft knife, cut along the outline. A sure, continuous line is best, so be confident. If you are tentative, the line will look jerky and show on the stencilled design. For long, curved lines, it is easier to move the board around as you work, rather than the blade.

BORDERS

These attractive border patterns can be used on a wall, door, piece of furniture or any other suitable item. Choice of colors depends on the room and the background color of the design. You can use a single color for simplicity, or choose a range of several contrasting colors. Alternatively, you might decide on a two-tone effect worked in a light and dark version of the same color. Pale colors can look effective on a dark background; dark colors are often enhanced by a lighter background. The finished effect depends

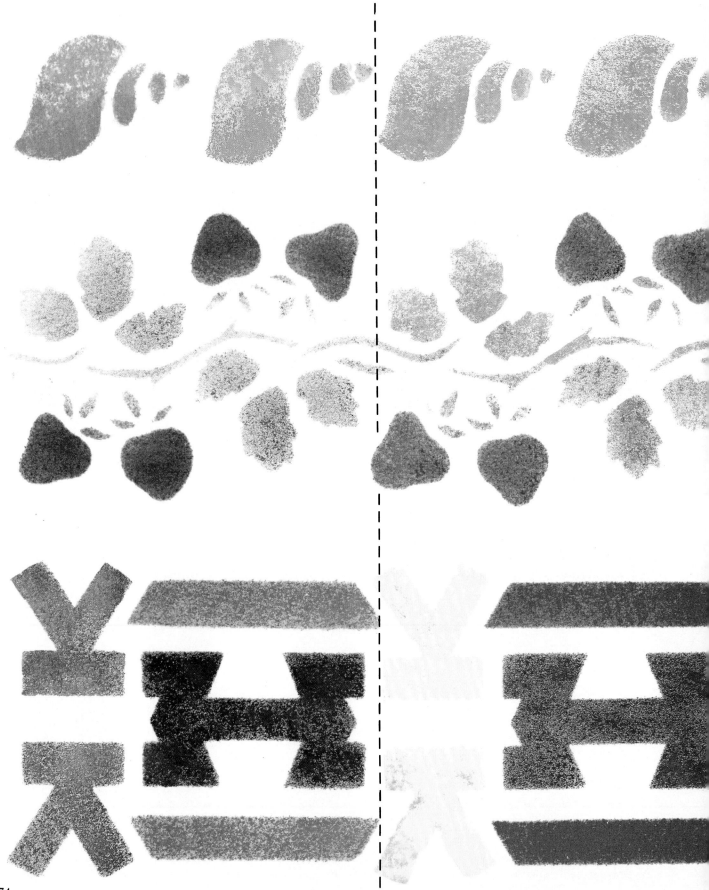

*entirely on your choice of colors,
so it is worth giving these some
though and even trying out a few
different color combinations on
pieces of scrap paper before you
begin stencilling.*

75

DESIGN IDEAS

◁ *An elegant geometric border stencil has been chosen to complement the proportions of this hallway. The depth of the crown molding stencil visually reduces the ceiling height and a more narrow stencil using part of the same motif links the chair rail to the crown molding.*

▽ *An informal continuous vine border has been placed deliberately to frame this dining area. Note how some of the details – grapes, figs and fig leaves – have been used individually to give extra dimensions to the border.*

Spray stencilling

*Spray paints are excellent for stencilling
and they can be used very successfully on all types
of surfaces, from walls and floors to furniture and
fabric. Here, spray paints and floral stencils have been used to
decorate fabric for curtains and a chair cover.*

One of the joys of stencilling is allowing the colors to overlap, to create a wonderfully shaded and muted effect. Spray paints are ideal for achieving these mellow effects: they can be applied lightly and, as they dry quickly, thin veils of color can be easily blended.

△ *Use the floral stencils, shown above, to transform plain sheets into charming, delicately-shaded furnishings to brighten a room.*

Stencilled fabric

When using spray paints, it is important to remember to use the paint very thinly, building up the colors gradually. Since the paint dries quickly there is no need to wait before adding the next color. Do not worry about color variations in the finished items, as this will add to the overall effect. When spray paints are used correctly, a subtle overlapping of color will enhance the final effect. If you want the colors to be more defined, cut separate masks for each color.

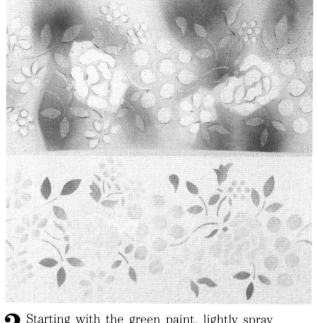

You will need

◇ Spray aerosol paint: we used dark green, light blue, dark blue, pale yellow and cherry red
◇ Stencil acetate
◇ Fabric: we used unbleached sheet
◇ Kitchen towel
◇ Masking tape

Method

1 Place the fabric on a clean, flat surface. Spray back of stencil with spray adhesive. Leave for a moment to become tacky to the touch; then position it on to the fabric and press down firmly, making sure that no gaps are left between the stencil and the fabric for the paint to seep underneath.

2 Carefully mask round the stencil with kitchen towel and masking tape to protect the surrounding fabric from the spray paint.

3 Starting with the green paint, lightly spray the leaves and foliage in the design, holding a piece of cardboard in your other hand to help direct the spray. Add touches of yellow and cherry red – leaves are seldom just green and adding other colors gives a natural, mellow look.

PATTERN EXTRA

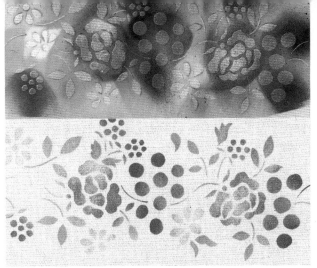

4 Spray the roses and daisies with pale yellow paint. To make the peach colored roses, spray a little cherry red on to the outer petals. To shade the color in this way hold your piece of cardboard round the edge of the rose to actually aim the paint at the base of the cardboard. In this way a little of the paint will be deflected onto the rose petals.

5 To shade the grapes, use some pale blue spray, followed by less of the dark blue; for luscious looking grapes add a little cherry red at outer edges. For brambles, use dark blue paint with a touch of cherry. During this, the daisies will have caught a little of each color and will blend in well.

6 Periodically lift a corner of the stencil to inspect your progress – the image will look stronger when the stencil is lifted. Once satisfied with the effect, remove the stencil. Re-apply adhesive and stencil the next section.

Border stencil

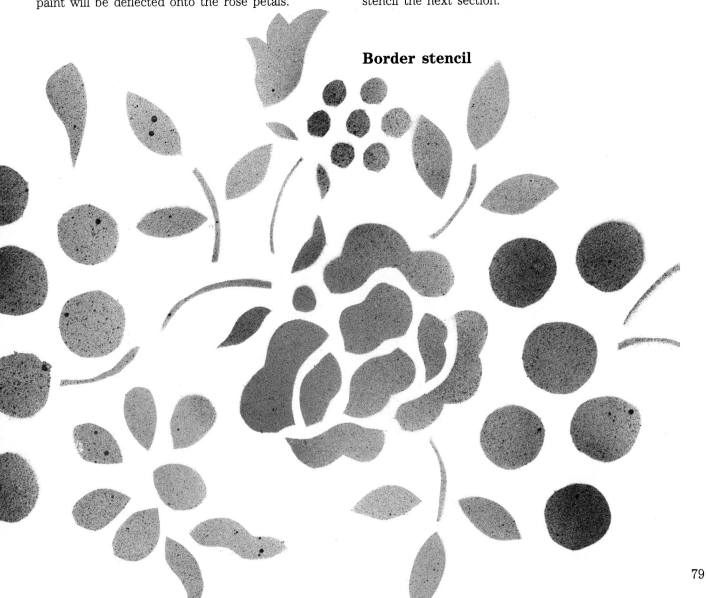

Circular stencil

$\triangleleft \triangle$ *This garland design was adapted from the border stencil on the previous page. To use the circular stencil, trace the pattern on to acetate, repeating some of the motifs to make a complete circle.*

$\triangleright$ *Use this individual motif to decorate small items or scatter it around a larger design.*

Individual motif stencil

81

Using spray paints

Spray paints come in a vast range of colors, though only a few cans are needed to create a wide spectrum of shades. The paint is acrylic-based and therefore dries almost instantly, enabling you to work more quickly. However, it is important to apply the paint evenly and very sparingly, otherwise unattractive, hard blocks of color could be formed. This is easy to judge: if the surface looks wet, too much paint is being used.

To use the paint, hold the can about 8in from the surface and, using a gently pumping action, spray in short bursts to give a thin layer of color. Hold a piece of cardboard in your other hand to help direct the spray and protect the rest of the stencil.

Before you start, perfect your technique by practicing on paper or spare scraps of fabric. This will enable you to see how the colors are going to work together. With practice, you will soon master the technique and gain confidence.

Suitable fabrics

All kinds of fabric can be stencilled, but always experiment first to ensure that you achieve the desired result. Natural fabrics are particularly nice to use as they absorb the paint well to produce lovely, soft colors that highlight the shaded areas.

Fabric that has been stencilled with aerosol spray paint must either be dry-cleaned or carefully hand washed in warm water and mild detergent. Do not wash the stencilled fabric in a washing machine as this will cause the colors to fade.

Cutting stencils in masks

With more complex stencils it is worthwhile cutting several stencils, or masks, for the various colors. This will enable you to work more quickly as there is no need to protect the different areas of the stencil from the individual colors being used. However, it is still important to shade the colors carefully to allow for some overlap of color, otherwise the result may appear too slick and rigid.

To repeat the stencil for each different color, lay the master stencil on a sheet of stencil film and use the spray paint to stencil a copy of the film. Repeat this to make as many masks as required, keeping each mask to one color of the pattern and only cutting out the motifs needing those colors. Make sure that you have

△ *When using aerosols, always wear a mask and work in a well-ventilated room. Protect areas not to be painted with paper and use cardboard to angle the spray.*

register marks on each stencil, to enable you to position each one accurately. Always work in the same sequence and lift off each mask as it is completed before positioning the next accurately.

Using the stencils

As with other stencilling methods, it is essential to stick the stencil firmly to the surface being painted: for the best results use a spray adhesive that enables you to reposition the stencil. Using an adhesive helps to prevent paint seeping under the stencil which will spoil the clean edge of the design.

Once the stencil is in position, surround it with paper towels, attached with masking tape. This will protect other areas from the drift of spray.

Design ideas

These informal, rather random floral designs are very adaptable and easy for the novice to use, as opposed to geometric patterns which require very careful positioning. The border design illustrated here can be used vertically or horizontally and just butted up where it turns a corner.

To transform a small room, use the border panel to decorate the walls at chair rail level or where the wall meets the ceiling. It would also make handsome tie-backs, which could be attached to curtains made from darker fabric which is less suitable to stencil.

The oval garland, used on the chair cover, would also look attractive stencilled on top of a chest of drawers or a small table. You could then use the border design across the drawer fronts and parts of the garland to make swags to decorate the sides.

Try combining both designs to transform large, plain curtains. Work a repeat pattern, with the oval garland placed between the stripes of the border design, across the width of the fabric.

The little posy design could be dotted about on walls inside the stencilled border to give a cottagey effect. Alternatively, use it inside a cupboard door or under the lid of a chest to give an unexpected, pleasing feature when the lid is opened.

Block printing

*Printing is simply the transfer of inks or dyes by
means of pressure. Block printing is the simplest form of
this craft and its great advantage is that it
can be used to produce very effective results at home – without
the need to buy any expensive equipment.*

Block printing

This simple and direct printing technique can be used on almost any surface. It is an ideal way to brighten up a plain wall or decorate a large piece of furniture, even to print a length of fabric.

Block printing has survived as an art form for over 2000 years, and part of the reason for this lies in its versatility. A variety of materials can be used to make the printing block ranging from wood and linoleum to string and crumpled paper. Another advantage of block printing is that you don't have to learn how to register a print – pleasing and dramatic effects can be created by using just one color. Don't be too ambitious at first, try printing a small area using a simple repeat pattern, before commiting yourself to the whole room or a pair of curtains or a bedspread.

Handprinting is always irregular, so don't worry if each printed motif looks different. These variations will add to the final effect. If, however, the surface you are printing on is uneven, a sponge block is by far the best because it is flexible enough to print over most uneven surfaces.

△ *The range of materials that can be used as the printing block is limited only by your imagination. Try experimenting with pasta shapes, pieces of string and crumpled tissue paper mounted on a block to create a variety of interesting textured prints.*

Tools and equipment

The basic materials required for block printing are very simple. Many of the items, such as a sharp blade or craft knife, glue and a paintbrush, you may well already have. You will also need:

Paint

You can use latex paint, artists' acrylics or children's finger paints. The latter are particularly good because they are relatively inexpensive and come in a range of bright colors. Acrylic dries quickly, and is therefore only suitable for small areas.

Whichever paint you use, it should not be too runny – the consistency of thick cream is about right. All the paints are water-based which makes cleaning up easy. For printing on fabric, use special fabric colors with an appropriate thickener and fix colors in place by ironing.

Blocks

Printing blocks can be made by either carving out a shape from the block or by mounting a textured surface on to the block to form a relief motif. One of the simplest forms of block printing is potato printing – a method often used to introduce the craft to children, but the technique can be easily adapted and upgraded to suit the most sophisticated tastes.

Traditionally wood, linoleum or heavy cardboard have been used to make blocks but other mediums can be used. Styrofoam and simple household sponges both make effective blocks with the added advantage that they are easy to carve.

The following pages demonstrate how to make block prints using an ordinary household sponge as the printing block.

Using a roller

Using a roller ensures that the paint is applied evenly to the relief surface. This is important as it avoids some parts of the printed design being very faint in appearance while others look clogged. Although slight variations in the density of the paint are part of the charm of block printing, it is worth taking some care to avoid the overall effect being too messy.

Printing surfaces

It is possible to print on most surfaces including fabric and wood, wool and paper.

Sponge printing

If you are working with single motif designs shaped from a sponge, or a block of sponge on a relatively small area, then mounting on wood is not necessary. This is the simplest method of block printing.

1 Draw the outline of your design with felt tip pen or pencil on to a synthetic sponge (a close-grained sponge gives a dense print, a coarser sponge produces a more textured effect). Use a sharp scalpel or craft knife to neatly cut away all the areas that you do not want to print.

2 Here the background area is cut away to produce a raised petal shape suitable for a random scattered design. A single motif can also be cut from the flat side of a halved potato.

3 To print, pour the paint into a shallow container and dip in the sponge, cut side down. Apply the block firmly to the surface to be painted, taking care not to smudge the design. One paint application should last for several prints.

4 To obtain a sharp edge to your design, stick a length of masking tape firmly to the surface before applying the paint. Take the printed color up to and over the tape. When the paint is dry, remove the tape to reveal the straight edge.

Mounting a sponge block

To make a sponge block last longer it can be mounted onto a thin piece of wood or heavy cardboard. Shape the sponge first, then glue it to the wood using a water-proof glue. The block will be easier to use if it has a handle on the back. This will also prevent you covering your hands with paint. An old cupboard handle, mounted onto the back of the block, makes an ideal handle. You could also use a smaller square of wood, glued in place on the back, as a handle.

▷ *Trace your design onto a sponge with a felt tip pen and use a sharp razor blade to cut away the areas you do not wish to print.*

△ *Mount the sponge block on to a flat piece of wood for easy handling. Here we have used a piece of wood with a wooden cupboard knob screwed to the back.*

△ *The paint can also be applied with a paint brush, although a roller will give a more even paint coverage. Apply the paint evenly to the relief surface. Make sure the paint you are using isn't too runny.*

▽ *A simple repeat pattern using just one color can produce very effective results. The sponge block gives a wonderfully textured print, that works well applied to a slightly textured surface like this wall.*

Painting on furniture

Transform ordinary furniture and shabby household objects into original works of art by painting them with bold geometric patterns and motifs. You don't need to be an expert artist to achieve pleasing results that will liven up your home.

Doors, chairs, cupboards, in fact any item in the home, can begin to look rather 'tired' with age and detract from the overall appearance of a room. Instead of replacing items or simply covering them with a coat of paint, why not create a bright and unusual scheme by painting them with original designs or motifs.

Freehand designs have a charm and appeal all of their own, which is far less structured than other decorative techniques like stencilling.

Don't worry if you cannot draw as you can still produce stunning results. Use everyday objects as templates for bold geometric designs or try copying the designs in books or even wallpaper designs if they are reasonably simple.

Materials and equipment

Many items such as sandpaper, rags, paper, pencil and scissors, you may already have at home. However, you will need to purchase brushes, varnish and paints to suit the surface to be painted.

Paints

The paint you choose will depend on the surface you are decorating.

Latex and acrylic paints These are used when painting on wood. Latex is inexpensive and ideal for covering large areas such as doors, wall panels and pieces of furniture. Artists' acrylics are more costly but come in a wide range of vibrant colors and are extremely tough and durable. It is possible to combine latex and acrylic paints. For example, it is often a good idea to paint large, background areas with latex, then paint the smaller motifs in bright acrylics. Alternatively, you can mix the two paints together as they are both water-based. Latex takes several hours to dry, whereas acrylic dries in a few minutes.

Ceramic paints When decorating tiles and other glazed surfaces use special ceramic paints. These are available from good art and craft shops. As these paints are not water-based, you must also buy a suitable thinner.

Metal paints Special paints and enamels are available for painting metal. Follow the manufacturer's instructions for thinning, preparation and drying time.

Varnishes

A coat of clear matt or gloss varnish protects the finished painted surface and will enhance the colors. In rooms likely to get splashed by water – bathrooms and kitchens – painted surfaces benefit from two or three coats of varnish. Table tops and other surfaces subject to wear and tear should also be protected with several coats of varnish.

Brushes

Choose a brush in a size that suits the area you wish to paint. Use decorating brushes to paint large areas. For small areas and intricate patterns use artists' brushes. Wash all brushes immediately after use. This is very important when using quick-drying acrylics because if this paint is allowed to dry on the bristles, the brushes will no longer be usable.

Preparation

Surfaces must be smooth and free from dirt and grease. Old paintwork should be washed thoroughly and rubbed down with sandpaper to remove loose particles of paint and roughen the surface – this enables the new paint to adhere to the old. Always prime new wood before applying a basecoat.

If there are any cracks or flaws in the surface, fill them with an appropriate filler, following the manufacturer's instructions. Then rub down with sandpaper before painting the basecoat.

Planning designs

Bold patterns and loosely painted motifs, such as those featured in this bathroom, are effective and easy to do. However, the success of this seemingly casual effect depends on careful planning. Both your design and color scheme must be carefully thought out before you start painting.

Plan your design on paper first, keeping it as simple as possible. Try basing the design on geometric shapes, such as ovals and circles, which can be adapted to create a wide variety of interesting shapes and designs.

Same-size designs

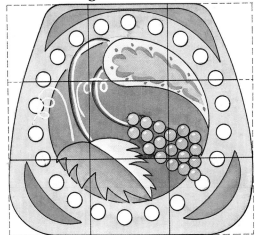

If you are painting a fairly small area, such as a chair seat, you can make a pencil drawing of your design on a piece of paper that is the same size as the chair seat.

To transfer the design to the seat, scribble over the back of the paper with a soft pencil, then position the paper on the chair, with the original design face up. Trace firmly over the original lines of the pattern – only draw the main outlines of the design as the details can be painted in later. Alternatively, transfer the design by drawing a grid over it and copying it, square by square, on to a similar grid drawn directly on to the chair seat.

Enlarging designs

If you are painting a large area, such as the side of a bath, it may be impractical to make a drawing of the same size. In this case, make a smaller drawing, in proportion to the area to be painted, and mark a grid over the top. To transfer the design, mark up the surface to be painted with the same number of squares but proportionately larger, then copy the design square by square onto the surface.

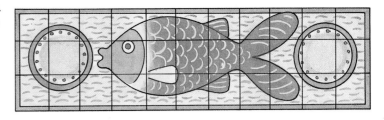

Using templates

When painting simple or repeated designs, you can save time by making a template. Cut your chosen shapes out of paper or cardboard and then draw around them on to the surface you are painting. Alternatively, create circles, ovals and squares by drawing around household objects such as dishes, plates and boxes.

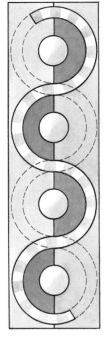

▷ *To make this continuous curved motif, first draw five circles using a template, then adapt them as shown here.*

△ *Simple designs are often the most effective of all. This floral design is built up from geometric shapes – a circle for the flower motif and curves for the leaves. Use plates as the templates.*

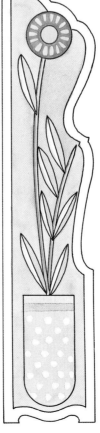

Freehand designs

Many designs can be painted directly onto your surface without the use of a template. However, it is still advisable to make a rough sketch first so that you are clear about the design before you begin.

If there are a lot of repeated shapes in the design it is a good idea to combine the use of templates with more original freehand images.

Choosing colors

Choice of color is very personal, however, whatever shades you choose to use, it is essential to plan the scheme carefully. Try experimenting on a piece of paper with different color combinations using other tones in the room as a base. If you wish to totally transform a room, make sure that you create a harmonious scene by creating a visual color link between the different items.

DESIGN IDEAS

▷ *A sideboard is given a new lease on life with a floral pattern to complement the existing decor.*

◁ *'Frame' a fireplace with your own picture painted onto surrounding tiles with ceramic paints. This hearth is a good example of breaking free from traditional fireplace colors and motifs.*

▽ *An aspect of a plain kitchen – the door – is used to advantage here for interest and warmth. One strutting grey chicken, artfully topped with red, brings life and humor to the room.*

Painting frames

*Decoratively painted frames can highlight
the prints and paintings they contain. A hand-painted
frame, specially designed to set off a favorite
picture, photograph or mirror, gives an enchanting finishing
touch to the decoration of a room.*

Turn prints, postcards, or even pages from magazines, into unusual pictures for your walls by mounting them in customized frames. Inexpensive wooden, metal and plastic frames can all be given the designer touch. All it takes is for you to paint them imaginatively, so that they complement and bring to

life the picture they hold.

Break all the rules of framing, which preach that the frame should play second fiddle to the picture, by making it part of the picture. This can be used effectively for inexpensive postcards or prints, that need an individual touch to loose their mass-produced look.

△ The design of this bright and cheerful painted frame has been inspired by the picture it holds. The colors and motifs of the abstract design were taken from a patterned tablecloth. They were then drawn on to the primed frame in pencil and painted, using bold primary colors.

◁ *The inspiration for the garden motif on this frame came from the leaves and flowers depicted in the print. These shapes were used as design ideas, but were simplified to form a repeat pattern of leaves around the frame. Soft pastel shades were used to complement the color of the vase and flowers.*

Design ideas

When decorating the frame, be inspired by the print you have chosen. For the easiest approach, pick out two colors in the print and paint simple motifs or abstract patterns. Stripes of repeated stencilled motifs, or dashes of color, work well. If the picture depicts a rural scene, use leaves and flowers as design ideas, but simplify them. For instance, decide on a shape and use this as a repeated pattern. The more adventurous may like to try recreating a section of the picture around the frame.

Colors

The joy of designing and painting your own frame comes from the satisfaction of achieving exactly the effect you want. Whether you use bold, striking color effects or subtle, pastel shades, bear in mind that the colors you choose for the frame should help to enrich those used in the picture.

For the best results, choose from colors that are used in the picture. For example, a bright red frame for a soft pastel print is unlikely to work, yet it may make a black and white photograph look striking.

Painting a mirror frame is particularly easy because the design can be as bold and bright as you like. If the mirror is a large one, and an important feature of a room, then choose colors that fit in with the way the room is decorated.

Choosing a picture

Select some printed matter that you particularly like, such as a postcard, a favorite greeting card, or a family photograph. This can be used as the inspiration for the decoration of the frame.

Selecting a frame

It does not matter if the frames are shabby or chipped because you can renovate them. You need to fill cracks and use sandpaper on the surface of all frames before painting them.

Plain, wooden frames are ideal for decorating because their porous texture absorbs paint easily. Hunt for cheap, wooden frames, or old discarded frames, as your imagination will transform them into something fresh and new. Metal, plastic and other materials also work well if the correct paints are used. Avoid ornate frames, because the result can look overdone.

▷ *The striking colors used to decorate this Impressionist-style frame were taken from the violets and blues in the print itself. The frame was painted with a background color, then dotted with a different color.*

Materials and equipment

Home decorators will already have some basic materials, such as wood filler and sandpaper which are needed to repair old frames. But, for a really decorative finish, visit your local art shop for a wide range of brightly colored paints.

Filler

Before priming the frame, fill all cracks and chips with a wood filler. Many frames, even new ones, have small gaps where the mitered corners meet. These should be filled and sanded so that the surface is even.

Primer

Once the surface of the wooden frames has been prepared, they must also be primed before being painted. Acrylic gesso is an ideal base because it gives a smooth, white finish.

Alternatively, you can apply two coats of white household latex paint to the frame before adding colors.

Paints

Acrylic paints are the most suitable paints for this type of decorative work, because they are hard-wearing and can be used on wood, metal, plaster and plastic. Available from most art shops, acrylics are water-based, quick-drying and come in a wide range of colors.

Latex water-based paint can be used on most frames but it is less durable than acrylic paint. It may get scratched or chipped when used on smooth surfaces, such as plastic, but it works well on wood.

Enamel paints can be used on metal, plastic and lacquered frames. They are available from craft or art shops. The drying times of different makes vary considerably, and many enamels have to be diluted with an appropriate thinner.

Varnish

Leave the frames to dry thoroughly once they have been painted. When dry, most painted frames should be sealed and finished with at least two coats of protective varnish. To seal acrylic and latex paints use either an acrylic varnish or a special acrylic medium, available from art shops. One exception is enamel paint, which has a hard, non-porous surface, and therefore does not need to be varnished.

Brushes

Depending on the design and the size of your frame, you will need a selection of brushes. A small water-color brush is essential for painting any fine details on the frames. One or two larger brushes are useful for painting broader areas of color. Use a small decorating brush for applying primer and varnish. Clean all brushes immediately after use.

Painting a wooden frame

Wooden frames are the easiest to use for a first project. Choose a picture that can be brought to life with a simple repeat pattern on the frame. Prime and seal the frame, and you are ready to paint.

You will need

◇ Acrylic paint in various colors
◇ Acrylic gesso in white
◇ Acrylic medium or acrylic varnish
◇ Selection of sable or hair artists' brushes
◇ Small decorator's brush
◇ Fine sandpaper
◇ Wood filler (putty)
◇ Palette or dishes for mixing paint

1 Fill any cracks or chips in the frame with wood filler. When the filler is dry, thoroughly rub down the frame with fine sandpaper.

2 Apply at least two coats of acrylic gesso or other primer, allowing each coat to dry before applying the next. If necessary, give the frame a rub down with sandpaper between coats.

3 Use a sharp pencil to draw the design onto the primed frame. Apply the paint one color at a time, allowing each color to dry before attempting to paint an adjoining color.

4 Finally, when the paint is dry, apply at least two coats of varnish to protect the paint.

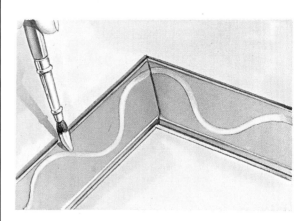

If the frame is flat, you can include the mitered corners into your design.

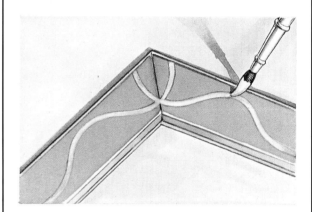

Alternatively, ignore the diagonal mitered lines and take your design to the edge of the frame.

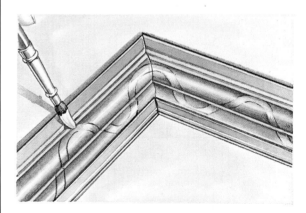

When painting a molded frame, the miters cannot be ignored. The design you choose must follow the contours and ridges of the molding and take into account the shape of the corners.

◁ *For a different look, try immitating Indian black lacquer. Paint the frame and mount black and draw the lines on with a gold felt-tip paint pen. Fill in the flowers on the mount with deep blue acrylic paint.*

INDEX

PHOTOGRAPHIC CREDITS
4-5 IPC Magazines/Robert Harding Syndication, 6 Elrose Products ltd, 7 Crown Paints, 8 EWA, 9(I) Crown Paints, 9(r) Mal Stone/Eaglemoss, 10 Crown Paints, 11 Living Magazine, 12-14 John Suett/Eaglemoss, 15 EWA/ Spike POwell, 16-17, 18(t) Ian Howes/Eaglemoss, 18(I) EWA/Andrea Von Einseidel, 18(r) Collins and Brown, 19 Steve Tanner/Eaglemoss, 20-22 Ian Howes/Eaglemoss, 25(b) Collins and Brown, 27-29 John Suett/Eaglemoss, 31 Steve Tanner/Eaglemoss, 35-38, 39, 41 100 Idees, 40 Martin Norris/Eaglemoss, 43 Modes et Travaux, 44, 45(I) 100 Idees, 47,48 Shona Wood/Eaglemoss, 49-52(t) Steve Tanner/Eaglemoss, 52(b) Bridgeman Art Library, 53 Fritz Von Der Schulenberg, 54 Steve Tanner/Eaglemoss,55-56 Modes et travaux, 57 Royal Pavillion, Brighton, 58 Garden Picture Library, 60(I) Martin Norris/Eaglemoss, 60(r) Toucan Books, 61 Freda Parker/Eaglemoss, 62 Bridgeman Art Library, 64(I) EWA/Frank Herholdt, 64(r) Simon Butcher/Eaglemoss, 65, 66 Zed Nelson/Eaglemoss, 67 Steve Tanner/Eaglemoss, 68(t) EWA/David Cripps, 68(b) Steve Tanner/Eaglemoss, 69 100 Idees, 70 Felicity Benyon Stencil Kits, 71 IPC Magazines/Robert Harding Syndication, 73 Steve Tanner/Eaglemoss, 76 Jon Bouchier, 77,78 John Suett/Eaglemoss, 83,84 100 Idees, 85 Crown Paints, 86 Collins and Brown, 87,88,89 Crown Paints, 90(t,br) 100 Idees, 90(bl) Houses and Interiors, 91,92,93 Steve Tanner/Eaglemoss, 94 Salamander Books.

Key: EWA = Elizabeth Whiting and Associates